Looking Back
100 YEARS —
100 ARTEFACTS
NIAGARA-ON-THE-LAKE

Interior of Memorial Hall in 1927

Photo taken from the upper gallery of Memorial Hall in 1927

Looking Back

100 YEARS — 100 ARTEFACTS

Niagara-on-the-Lake

Niagara Historical Museum

Looking Back Press

Copyright © 2007 by Niagara Historical Museum. All rights reserved. No part of this book may be reproduced, stored in a retrieval system, or transmitted in any form without written permission of the publisher.

Vanwell Publishing acknowledges the financial support of the Government of Canada through the Book Publishing Industry Development Program for our publishing activities.

Published by Looking Back Press
An Imprint of Vanwell Publishing Limited
1 Northrup Crescent, P.O. Box 2131
St. Catharines, ON L2R 7S2
For all general information contact Looking Back Press at:
Telephone 905-937-3100 ext. 829
Fax 905-937-1760
E-Mail vanessa.mclean@vanwell.com

For customer service and orders:
Toll-free 1-800-661-6136

Printed in Canada

National Library of Canada Cataloguing in Publication

Niagara Historical Museum
100 Years-100 Artefacts : Niagara-on-the-Lake
ISBN 978-1-55068-954-1

1. Niagara-on-the-Lake (Ont.)--History--Exhibitions.
2. Material culture--Ontario--Niagara-on-the-Lake--Exhibitions.
3. Niagara Historical Museum--Catalogs. I.Title. II.Title:One hundred years - one hundred artefacts.

FC3099.N54A25 2007   971.3'38   C2007-904336-4

Acknowledgements

The Niagara Historical Society is indebted to the work of the 100 contributors to this community project. Their names are identified with their submissions. Without them, *100 Years – 100 Artefacts* would not have been possible.

The work that goes into such an ambitious project requires many people. In order to contact 100 individuals to assist with a project like this, it is necessary to have many people who believe in the work of the institution, and we thank them for it. Sheila Tierney, Terry Mactaggart, co-chairs of the centennial celebrations, convinced a large number of individuals that this was a unique opportunity.

The editors of this project, Donald Combe, Fred Habermehl and Andrew Panko, reviewed the submissions to ensure that the voices of their authors were not lost and that the publication flowed smoothly and consistently.

Finally, we would like to thank Andrea Field for her photography work on the project. Her photos grace pages 9, 11, 12, 14, 20-25, 27-45, 47-73, 76-81, 83, 84, 86, 88-90, 93, 96, 100, 102, 104-108, 110 and 115.

100 Years — 100 Artefacts
is sponsored by
Barb and Ed Werner

Preface

"A meeting will be held in the Public Library on Thursday evening, December 12, 1895, at 7:30 p.m. to take steps to organize a Historical Society for Niagara. A cordial invitation is given to all interested in the subject to be present."

Thus a humble gathering of fifteen individuals led to the founding of the Niagara Historical Society.

By 1903 these guardians of history, under the determined leadership of Janet Carnochan, who were building both a reputation and a collection, proposed a monument to the memory of the Loyalist settlers of Niagara. On June 4, 1907 the first building in Ontario designed solely for use as a historical museum opened its doors. The structure designed by the sculptor Walter Allward, who would later fashion the Canadian Memorial at Vimy Ridge, was described in the local press as "a commodious structure of red brick, with white brick facings, situated on Castlereagh Street facing the military ground and is admirably suited to its purpose."

Naming the building was a new challenge, as we learn from reports at the time: "Several names have been suggested, the UEL Memorial, Memorial of the War of 1812, then a suggestion to call it simply Memorial Hall, it would thus be in memory of the United Empire Loyalist who landed here, it may be in memory of the Regiments, British and Canadian who have fought here, or it may be in memory of the early settlers of whatever land, or of the business men who helped to make Niagara an important Town, in short it may be a memorial of whatever great or good has been here in the past."

Thus it became Memorial Hall. It is now a Museum consisting of three independent buildings merged together, Memorial Hall (1907), the High School (1875) and the Link Building (1971). Reaching the Centenary mark of such a place is cause for celebration. However, rather than celebrate the bricks of the house, the staff of the Niagara Historical Society suggested "100 Years – 100 Artefacts" as a theme, to be published as collection of stories about key artefacts in an extraordinary collection.

What better way to celebrate than to transform the artefacts of history into the stories of history, stories as diversified as their authors. Some say historians tell their stories as troubadours had offered their songs. Others say history is simply gossip, or fables not quite agreed upon. We, however, feel each author has observed and researched his or her presentation to tell us what happened and will leave to the scholars to explain why it happened.

We have dedicated this book to the Community of Niagara-on-the-Lake, the seat of the first capital of Upper Canada, and say thank you to the one hundred authors that have made it possible.

Kelly M. James
Society President
Niagara-on-the-Lake, Ontario

100 Years

When Memorial Hall opened in 1907 it was centrally located across from Camp Niagara and next to the High School. The top photograph shows the Hall in its early years. The photo below shows the building on the edge of town facing Camp Niagara, a training facility for troops from across Southern Ontario.

Memorial Hall, 2007.

100 Artefacts

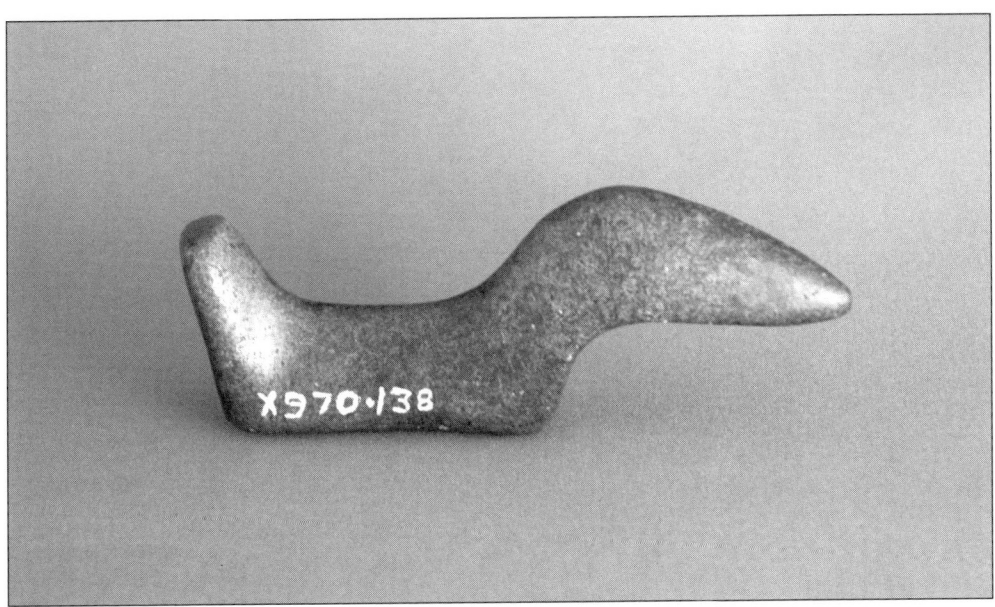

Birdstone

It is generally accepted that birdstones (other animal effigies have been found but are rare) are Algonkian in origin and made their first appearance within the Late Archaic and Early Woodland periods, or 3000-4000 years before present (B.P.), and that their production and use had ended completely before Late Woodland times or 2500 years B.P. The majority are made of glacial deposits of Huronian slate. Their distribution seems to be in the northeastern United States and southern Ontario.

The first step in creating a birdstone was the careful selection of a piece of stone. The general shape was attained by a hewing and flaking process by percussion, followed by a more gentle pecking process with a harder rock. Coarse grinding followed, and flint knives may have been used to scrape and plane the surface. Finely grained and powdered abrasives were used to finish and polish the birdstones.

The final step was the drilling of a vertical conical hole, met by a horizontal hole at each end of the flat base, using flint drills or copper awls with powdered quartz as an abrasive. The question of their purpose and use remains unanswered. It has been theorized that they were used as weights on atlatls, which were devices used to increase the power of a thrown spear. A second theory maintains that a birdstone was tied to the atlatl and used as a handle.

However, the craftsmanship and time involved in their creation makes it more probable that birdstones were amulets or ceremonial objects. (971.324)

by Ron Reimer

Paymasters Strong Box

The first time I can remember being inside our Museum I was about nine years old. In those days it was still much as it looked in many of the interior photographs taken in the early 1900s, showing enormous wood and glass showcases stuffed full of all kinds of artefacts. There were boxes on the floor and under the tables. I remember one filled with arrowheads and spear points.

One item always fascinated me: a huge iron military strongbox with wide iron bands, vertical and horizontal over and under each other on all sides and on top. The box measures thirty-two inches by twenty-four inches by twenty-two inches. Two men have some difficulty moving it. We think it weighs about four hundred pounds.

This interesting money chest has a secret. I first discovered it as a curious young boy – it has a hidden keyhole. There is a unique sliding section, rivet and all, that covers the keyhole. I have never forgotten this.

Years later I often tried to find the secret sliding rivet and could not, and a former Curator said it did not exist. About a year ago, Clark Bernat, Managing Director of the Museum and I, examined the box more closely and suddenly it was obvious. We found it – the sliding section moved. The keyhole appeared; I had not imagined the secret keyhole after all.

Soon after, for display, I made a full-scale wooden working mock up of the keyhole cover to show how it works.

The type of strongbox is probably British and earlier this year we found out that Fort Niagara has two similar strongboxes but of different sizes – with hidden keyholes. That part is still a secret yet to be uncovered. (986.1.55) **by Christopher Allen**

Niagara Historical Society Publications #1 - #44

As soon as the Niagara Historical Society was founded, this group of amateur historians began publishing booklets. They provided accounts of the indignities suffered during the Revolutionary War and the War of 1812. One issue published lists of names gathered from odd sources, an invaluable reference back to other primary documents. We are the heirs of this legacy, not only of their many publications, but of their urge to set down their stories in writing.

The researcher often feels a love/hate relationship with these early writers. One cannot do work in the history of Niagara-on-the-Lake without consulting their writings, but anyone who uses them suffers the frustration of discovering how much they omit. For example, they record that three officers were killed in battle in 1813 and lie buried in St. Mark's cemetery, but they provide no clue to the location of these graves. Equally frustrating, we learn that Domenic Henry was an old soldier of Cornwallis and one of the defenders of Long Island in the Revolutionary War and that he lies buried in this same cemetery, but without any hint of the grave site.

In spite of this lack of detail, we are indebted to the foresight of these early members of the Society for writing things down. Not only have they provided us with information about the past as remembered by their contemporaries, but they have set us an example of the importance of recording everything.

by Fred Habermehl

Butler Homestead Key

Keys have always intrigued me. What would they reveal if you found the locks they would open? This 18th century ancient, weary and worn key that belonged to Colonel Butler emits a delicious scent of past intrigues. What secret door will it open?

I imagine a charming room, a lady's room with a window seat, secret compartments, and billowy muslin curtains. Could it be, perchance, the boudoir of the Colonel's mistress? No! It's his daughter's room. She slept in her own room, separate from her four brothers.

Maybe it's not that kind of room, but it's the key to his wine cellar. Now that's a key he would not entrust to anyone. He would always have it on him – so why was it found buried in the dirt around his homestead? Or maybe, just maybe, it is the key to his strong box that held all the Loyalist documents he gathered before he fled to Canada in 1775 during the Revolutionary War.

Whatever this key was meant for, it was cherished because it would not have survived to this day to find its resting place in what I consider to be a wonderful, perfect, little museum. Perhaps, one day we will find the lock that it opens. (2000.011)   **by Bluma Appel**

> 2/h   Nov. 3 1845.
> Received from T.H. Johnson the sum of ___ Pounds, two Shillings and Six Pence, Provincial Currency, being for conveying John Harris to Gaol.
> Witness
> William [his X mark] Riley

Receipt for William Riley,

As one who is interested in the collection of Canadian black history, I have discovered over the past years the wealth of information Niagara has to offer. Much information has been gathered about the early community in Niagara that had its beginnings following the American Revolution, when black loyalists settled in the area after receiving land grants for their loyalty to the Crown.

There were many stories portraying the desperate circumstances of black pioneers and the indignities suffered due to their situation. Many newcomers to the land required time and effort in order to improve their family conditions, as did black citizens.

A great deal of the information we have gathered concerning blacks of Niagara has come from third-person stories. While on a recent visit to the Niagara Historical Museum I was surprised and pleased to be shown a document dated November 3, 1845. The document stated that a black man, William Riley, had been paid a stipend to escort a prisoner, John Harris, to the jail and it was signed by T.H. Johnson.

Being a witness to this small positive story with original proof gave me the confidence to carry on the mission of the Niagara Black Historical Society, of collecting the history showcasing the contribution of black Canadians to building their communities. (2001.324)

by Wilma Morrison

The Niagara Foundation

The Niagara Phoenix C.L. respectfully invites the attendance of Mrs. E. Lethworth and guests to dine at the Town Hall, Niagara-on-the-Lake at 8 o'clock P.M., Tuesday, Dec. 10. '63, in commemoration of the burning of Niagara, precisely 150 years to a day ago and the subsequent re-birth of the first capital of Upper Canada.

Niagara Foundation Artefacts - Newsletter and Dinner Invitation

The Niagara Historical Society has the first newsletter sent out by the Niagara Foundation in 1966, describing the Foundation's activities for its first four years of operation. As a private organization, the Foundation hoped to carry out projects not suitable for traditional organizations. By 1966, the Foundation had spearheaded Niagara's first official plan and inventory of historic buildings, restored the carriage in which the Duke of York toured Niagara in 1901, conducted an annual house tour which has continued since 1964, helped Niagara's merchants restore their historic store fronts, purchased Field's Drug Store (ultimately restored by the College of Pharmacy as the Niagara Apothecary), published the authoritative *Early Architecture of the Town and Township of Niagara* by Peter John Stokes, CRA, and staged celebrations for the 150th anniversaries of the Battle of Queenston (October 13, 1812) and the burning of Niagara (December 10, 1813, the "Niagara Phoenix"). The Society also has in its collection a 1963 invitation to a dinner commemorating the Niagara Phoenix, pictured here.

There are many similarities between the Society and the Foundation. Both began as not-for-profit citizen's groups to further Niagara's history and culture. Today, the Society's main focus is the operation of Niagara's museum. For its part, the Foundation continues with its annual house tour and the restoration of the William Stewart Homestead, an 1835 house built by William Stewart, an early black settler in town. The Foundation has also been a substantial contributor to the Society's fundraising campaigns. (2002.052.002 & 995.223)

by Tony Doyle

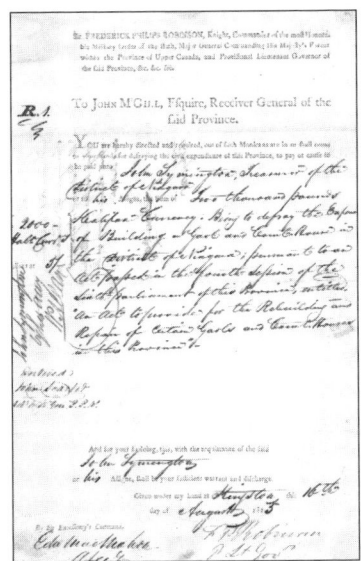

Warrant for the 1817 Court House

This warrant, measuring 19.5 by 32 cm, was signed by Sir Frederick Philips Robinson, Provisional Lieutenant-Governor of Upper Canada. It directs Receiver General John McGill to provide £2,000 in Halifax currency for the building of a new jail and courthouse in the Niagara District.

Retreating American forces had burned down most of the buildings in the Town of Niagara in 1813 during the War of 1812. One was the first jail and courthouse in the present area of King and Prideaux Streets. By 1815 the war was over, law and order needed to be maintained, and a new jail and courthouse were required.

It was to be built on land in the present Rye, Niagara and Charlotte Street area, donated by William Dickson, the noted local lawyer and politician. It would be out of the range of cannon fire from Fort Niagara, but Dickson, who owned other land in the area, would have probably seen the potential of a new public building leading to development on his other lands. A contemporary observer in 1818, however, wondered why such a magnificent building was set in a "swamp."

The courthouse was the seat of justice in Niagara from 1816 until the late 1860's. A number of key trials took place here, including that of reformer Robert Gourlay in 1819, the trial for thirteen 1837 rebels who were condemned to death (most of whom were reprieved), and trials of a further assortment of debtors, horse thieves, murderers, and the like. The jail housed many convicted (and accused) criminals, staged many executions and floggings, and sent many to the pillory.

In 1869 after a new courthouse was erected on Queen Street in the Town, the building was purchased by Maria Rye and renamed "Our Western Home." It was a home for young girls from England who, in the view of the time, had a better chance for a good life in Canada than in the orphanages or amongst the poor families in England. Its use changed over time and it was finally demolished in the 1970's. Its location is marked by an Ontario Heritage Trust plaque.

This 1815 warrant, which prescribed the construction of the building, is an important document not just for scholars of the history of early Ontario, but for those who are interested in the legal history of Niagara. (2002.060.001)   **by Robert Welch**

The Banner of the Loyal Canadian Society, Grimsby, Canada West, 1853

The inaugural dinner of the Loyal Canadian Society on October 13, 1847, pledged loyalty to the Queen, then honoured the memory of Major-General Sir Isaac Brock in "solemn silence." That tradition, starting at Randall's Hotel, Grimsby, lasted 37 years. Several founding members recalled that bitter-sweet day when, as young militiamen, they followed their leader into the murk of weather and war at Queenston, and emerged with a patriotic excitement for their land, and their hero. They proposed that the Loyal Canadian Society welcome all within its pale from whatever clime, the only test being that of a true and loyal Canadian subject. With an egalitarian membership of up to 200 persons, Society dinners were not military affairs, though they followed the form.

On October 13, 1853, the Society attended the re-interment of Isaac Brock at Queenston Heights. Society members marched proudly behind a banner made especially for that occasion. Thereafter, the banner occupied a place of honour at the dinner.

The 1853 banner depicts painted detail on red silk measuring five feet by five feet without the blue fringe. After 1884, the banner remained with the Nelles, U.E., family of Grimsby. Subsequently, the Society loaned the banner to the Lundy's Lane Historical Society, and then the Niagara Historical Society which finally assumed ownership. The banner's present condition is poor.

By 1956, the Queenston Dinner, Niagara-on-the-Lake, revived the Society's dinners in sentiment and form. Today, linking the present with the past, small copies of the Society banner grace the Head Table. (2003.043.009) **by Colin Duquemin**

1955 World Scout Jamboree Badge

The World Boy Scout Jamboree of 1955 was a unique event in the military history of the Commons (formerly the Fort George Military Reserve). It took place in the sweltering days of August of that year when 11,000 Scouts from 68 countries converged on this historic green. "Jamboree" is a Zulu word meaning "happy gathering," and this was the first one to be held outside of Europe – hence the motto: "New Horizons."
Lady Baden Powell, widow of the Founder of the Boy Scouts, was in attendance at the opening ceremonies. The Commons and the adjoining oak grove were filled with tents and the hustle and bustle was exciting to behold.
My personal connection to this event was a powerful one. I was a young wife and mother of two, living in Niagara Falls. My husband, a former Hungarian Eagle Scout, was delighted with this convergence of so many of his former mates. We were in attendance for at least 8 out of the 10 days of the event. Every evening, after a hurried dinner, we drove to Niagara in our rented car. We sat in the bleachers and watched the shows put on by scouts from various countries. Afterwards, we mingled with them among the tents. I still have the black and white photo of my year and a half old son, looking somewhat askance at the East Indian scout holding him in his arms.
The badge was given to each participant of the Jamboree. (2005.002.001) **by Clara Tarnoy**

Canning Factory Photograph

Canadian Canners Ltd., Aylmer Factory #13

As shown in the staff photographs, the canning factory provided seasonal employment for hundreds of local and imported workers.

Staff included Mrs. John Lavell, Forelady; Mr. A.C. Awde, Manager, and family; Pete Marino; Scoop McCarthy, Pipe-fitter; and Jessie Goodridge. A later manager was Cec Ward. Mr. Chambers, Stationary Engineer, was at the corner keeping the steam up, often firing in a load of peach pits.

Our family home was a brick house at the corner of Mary Street, facing the wooden quarters for out-of-town staff with its long gallery, useful for hanging laundry or just socializing. The pay-night parties went on pretty late. One night, unable to sleep, we went over. Fires were lit, jugs were passed around, an accordion played for dancing on the rickety gallery floors and there was a delicious smell of cooking chickens – ours from our coop. Our whole family worked at the cannery at times, while I sneaked in to watch the cans chuting down from above, the belts and machinery, the steaming basins of tomatoes or peaches, the shouts to "pick up" where there was a pile-up.

In its metamorphosis as a fashionable hotel, can the canning factory be any more exciting?

(2005.007.025) **by Margo Fyfe**

John Harris Clock

This tall case clock was made in England, and the style of the case would suggest a southern origin. The brass movement is a weight driven 30-hour time and strike mechanism with a seconds bit and calendar disk. There are no maker's marks on the clock, but the case and movement are dated to c1800. The clock belonged to John Harris, who lived in the Town of Niagara from 1826 to 1837.

John Harris was born in Worcester, England in 1787 and apprenticed as a baker. After the death of his first wife, he emigrated to Canada in 1818. It is possible that he brought the clock with him at that time. The following year he moved to Newton, New Jersey where he met and married his second wife, Margaret.

In 1826 John, Margaret, and their four children moved to the Town of Niagara where John opened a bakery. Mr. Harris was very active in the building of St. Vincent de Paul church and he held a number of positions in the parish including church warden. In 1837 John decided to sell his bakery business and he retired to a 226-acre farm near Guelph.

In 1854 his daughter Sarah Harris entered the Loretto Sisters order, and in 1864 she became Mother Superior at the Loretto Academy in Niagara Falls. John donated the clock to the Academy at this time. In 2005 the Academy was slated for redevelopment, and through the efforts of a descendant, the clock was donated to the Niagara Historical Museum. (2005.030.001)

by Richard Taylor

Canadian General Service Medal Fenian Raid 1870

In 1859 two Irish exiles came to America and brought their hatred of the British with them. It was this hatred that gave birth to a revolutionary secret society called the Fenian Brotherhood. Their aim was to destroy English rule in Ireland and establish an Irish Republic. Later it became an open society spreading to the United States, Canada, Australia and South America. The incursions into Canada from 1860-1870 were designed to cut off part of the British Empire. Their goal was to gain independence from Britain. Those who took part in the suppression of the Fenian Raids, according to NOTL resident Harold Clement, were rewarded with a medal. In 1899 his grandfather, J.P. Clement of Virgil, was one of the recipients of the medal. It was awarded to members of the Imperial and Canadian forces who had active service in the field, served as a guard or been detailed for some specific duty.

J.P. Clement was a farmer on Creek Road in Virgil. He was born in 1839 and died in 1918; he was married to Elizabeth Zimmerman. He was a corporal of the Canadian Queenston Mounted Infantry assigned to patrol the Niagara River.

This medal was reported missing in the 1930s, to be recovered in 2006 by the Museum. For Harold Clement the reappearance of the medal reminds him of his father's promise: "If it ever turns up, it's yours" and with Harold's loyal feelings to Niagara he is happy the medal has finally come home. (2006.008.001)   **by Selina Appleby & Harold Clement**

McClelland's West End Store Sign

The Mystery of the "T"

If you had lived here around 1875, you would have bought your groceries at McClellands, at the southwest corner of Queen at Victoria, under the sign of the "T." Your parents would have remembered when Lewis Clement built the store in 1834. They watched deliveries hoisted by pulley through the loading door above the entrance.

Maybe you were there when the big T sign was installed covering that loading door (inset). That was when McClellands turned the upstairs into living quarters.

Your children would have seen that sign being covered by a newer model – the new giant T and the words "West End Store". "McClellands" printed on the awning below identified the store until the late 1980s when the business moved.

Today your grandchildren can look above 106 Queen and see the third sign of the T. They may ask what it stands for. You may try the following answers:

T was the sign for provisions but ... Did every grocer use the T? ... Why a T? ... Perhaps tea was expensive and not everyone stocked it? ... Did some provisioners pay tax on tea or with tea, to the Crown? ... Was it only that T looked like the scale for weighing provisions?

Perhaps the mystery will be solved by a reader. Bring documentation to the Niagara Historical Museum and help solve The Mystery of the T. (2006.009.001)   **by Gail Nagley**

Tuning Box from Methodist Church

This wonderful little box was owned by Andrew Brady of the Methodist Congregation in the Old Town. Father Brady was a Methodist Class Leader who died in 1875. Music was an important aspect of life in the church. By the 1850s music was essential to the service. In the 1850s Mrs. Whitelaw played the melodeon, Mr. Varey Sr. the bass viol and George Varey the flute. The congregation also had a choir, for which this tuning box was essential. The tuning box comes in two pieces. The outer box is rectangular in shape and had a flat mouthpiece of ivory at the end that Mr. Brady would blow into. The secondary piece slides to control the pitch; this has handwritten notes on the slide.

In 1852 the Canada Presbyterian Church, often known as the Free Church, built a dignified brick building on Victoria Street. This Free Church ceased operation in 1869 and the Methodists decided to rent the building. In 1875 they bought it for $1,600.00. The former Methodist Meeting House was sold and moved, now a private home at the corner of Gate and Prideaux.

The Methodist Meeting House never owned any instrument more sophisticated than a melodeon. When the Methodists moved to the brick church on Victoria Street, the melodeon was hauled up with ropes into the gallery where Emily and Salome Burns played it.

By 1897 a small pipe organ had been installed which had to be pumped by hand. In 1924, a larger pipe organ was bought and the present organ was brought from Toronto in 1957.
(969.38) **by Mary Snider**

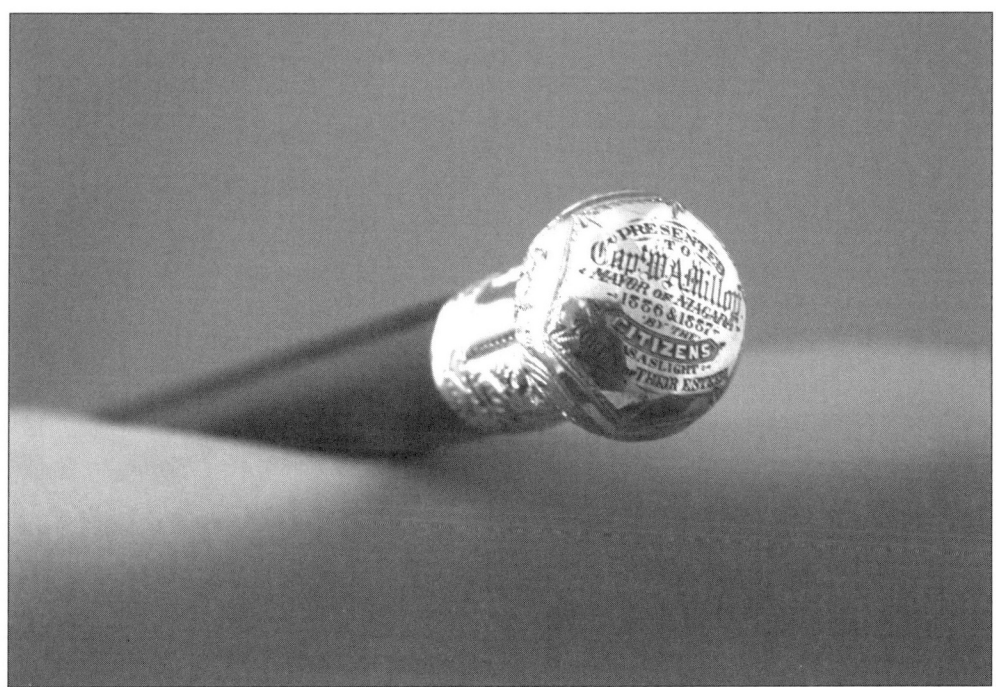

Swagger Stick

A museum, well-stocked with meaningful mementos of our past, has a positive influence on the lives of our residents, going far beyond what the written word and pictures can deliver. The opportunity to see something with one's own eyes adds another critical dimension to our appreciation of past history.

That is why I am pleased to donate this item, a walking stick that belonged to Captain William Milloy (son of Captain Duncan Milloy), to the Niagara Historical Museum in this, its 100th year. The connections between my own life, the life of Captain Milloy, and the Museum's anniversary are quite remarkable to me.

He was born in 1849, I was born almost 100 years later, in 1945. In 1895, he converted his family's private residence at 160 Front Street into the Oban Inn and operated it with his mother for many years. My mother purchased the Oban in 1962 and my family ran it for over 35 years.

William Milloy served as Mayor of Niagara-on-the-Lake for a two-year term, 1886–1887. I am now in my third term as Lord Mayor and can certainly appreciate the respect Captain Milloy enjoyed from the residents of Niagara-on-the-Lake, as witnessed by the engraving on the handle of the walking stick, which reads, "Presented to Capt W.A. Milloy, Mayor of Niagara 1886 & 1887 by the citizens as a slight token of their esteem."

I hope that visitors to the Museum enjoy viewing the walking stick and the story behind it. (2007.008.001) **by Lord Mayor Gary Burroughs**

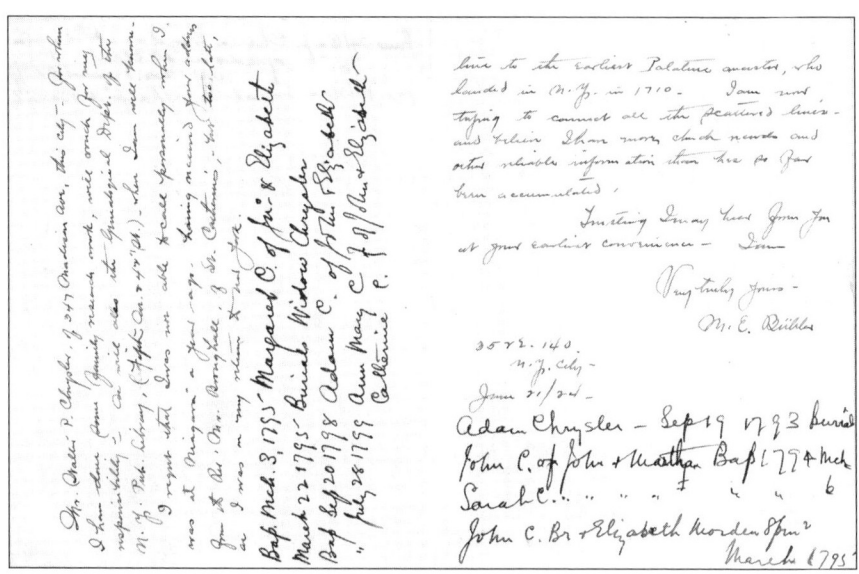

Letter to the Rector of St. Mark's Church

A folded sheet of stationery bears a handwritten letter on three pages, with notations on all four pages. The letter, dated June 21/24, addressed to the Rev. C.H.E. Smith, requests copies of Church records of the Crysler (Chrysler) family. The writer, M.E. Bühler of New York City, states that he understands that a "branch of the old N.Y. Tory family lived for awhile in your parish." He gives as his references the Genealogical Department of the New York Public Library and "Mr. Walter P. Chrysler of 247 Madison Ave., this city, for whom I have done some work." He adds: "I have traced the Canada line to the earliest Palatine ancestor, who landed in N.Y. in 1710."

Notations are of the 1793 burial of Adam Chrysler and of later burials and baptisms of his family prior to 1800. Also, two more recent baptisms are listed. Other notations are the dimensions of a 14-foot, 5-inch high window, and the phone numbers for a Stamford Lock Mfg. Co. and two others, possibly locksmiths.

Cryslers in Niagara are descendants of Johan Philip Greisler who came to New York in 1710 from the Heidelberg area of the Austrian Palatine in today's Germany (records in the Niagara-on-the-Lake Public Library include 44 alternative spellings of the family name). Johan Philip's grandson, Adam, farmed in the New York Catskills on Breakabean Creek, which flows via the Schoharie and Mohawk Rivers into the Hudson. During the American Revolution, Adam, who worked well with Natives, became a lieutenant in the British Army Indian Department. He and Native allies supported Butler's Rangers' raids. He later settled near St. Davids where he died in 1793. His Loyalist brothers also settled in Upper Canada.

Walter Percy Chrysler, 1875-1940, was also descended from Johan Philip Greisler. Walter's great great grandfather William became the first permanent resident of Chatham, Ontario. His grandfather moved to Kansas where Walter was born. Walter, a railroad engineer, became an automotive pioneer. He was president of Buick when it merged into General Motors. While still heading Buick, he became GM Vice President, Production. By 1924, he had left GM to try to revive the Overland and Maxwell automobiles. The latter melded into his new Chrysler Corporation. Walter is also remembered for saying: "If you pay enough money [the genealogists] can link you to Jesus Christ."   **by Robert Waugh**

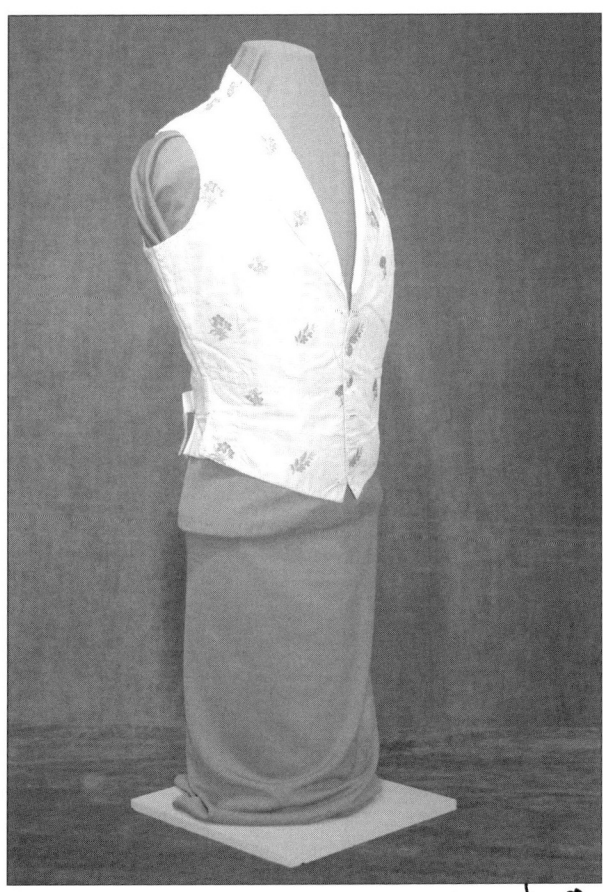

Plumb Waistcoat

This is a vest of corded silk attributed to Josiah Burr Plumb, a noted politician from Niagara. It is hand sewn of very fine cream silk with a random pattern of green flowers. It has soft padding and a cream coloured lining of muslin. The back is also of muslin and has a small belt. The front of the vest was adorned with six small brass buttons with fine etching, of which only three remain intact. It was designed with a soft shawl collar and three small pockets. There are two pockets at the waist and a breast pocket on the left side.

Josiah Burr Plumb was a Speaker of the Upper House at the time of his death in Ottawa in 1888. He was born in East Haven, Connecticut in May of 1846. After a successful career he immigrated to the Niagara region in 1865. He was married to Elizabeth Street, the daughter of a prominent businessman, Samuel Street Jr. of Chippawa. They had a family of three sons and three daughters.

In 1874, Plumb was elected MP for the county of Niagara. He was a hard working and loyal member of Sir John A. MacDonald's parliament. Therefore when he lost the general election in 1882 he was promptly appointed to the Senate, in February 1883. He proved to be so popular and successful in the House that he was elected as the Senate House Leader in 1887.

The condition of this garment is quite fragile as it is has many holes and stains. Its former glory can still be imagined. (972.221) **by Deborah Paine-Corbiere**

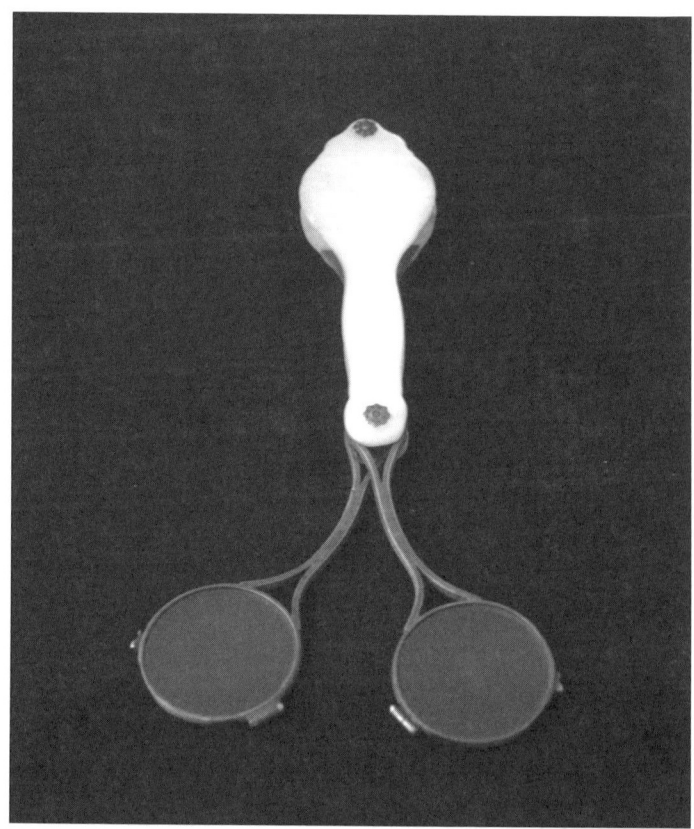

Eyeglasses

It was 1818, and William was late for lunch because he couldn't find his glasses. He thought they were probably buried beneath one of the piles of papers at either the Town Courthouse and Gaol on Rye Street, where he was Deputy Clerk, or the Stationery Store he managed on Queen Street. As he rushed home he thought how fortunate he was to have built his home at the corner of Mary and Regent Streets, half way between his two jobs and about the same distance from St. Andrew's Church where he was an elder. Dear Ann, his wife, would be waiting with lunch for him and their four impatient children would be getting restless with hunger. Little did he know that they would have a family of twelve children by 1832.

How would he tell Ann that he had lost his glasses again? He couldn't bear the thought of waiting months to have the lorgnettes replaced. Hopefully, they could be bought in York, not ordered from France where they were developed about 1780. The unique style had the two lenses attached at one side to a mother-of-pearl handle. He could fold the lenses into the handle for safe storage. However, the smaller size made it easier to misplace.

His friends teased him mercilessly because they were a style used mostly by women. He said they were Ann's and he was just borrowing them until his new ones arrived. Oh dear, maybe they'd turn up before he had to confess to Ann. (969.176) **by Terry & Terry Mactaggart**

Niagara Harbour and Dock Company Ledger Book

The Niagara Wharf Daily Register, 1836-1838, is the oldest of four surviving wharfage and storage registers from the Niagara Harbour & Dry Dock Company.

It is a brown leatherbound book measuring approximately 22x32x3cm. The spine of the book is severely worn, reflecting its day-to-day use. It contains approximately 100 pages with printed blue horizontal lines with red vertical lines that demark columns for dates, entries, and figures.

Entries (now brown with age) were hand written by several, mostly unidentified, authors. Most of the swirling script is legible and fairly easy to interpret. Entries were made in traditional British monetary denominations (pounds, shillings and pence). The ledger documents activity at the dock from November 1, 1836 through all of 1837 and up to the end of November 1838.

The Register documents daily income and disbursements for use of the dock facilities by various shippers, merchants and farmers, and "harbor dues" paid by boats or ships calling at the port, such as "Steamboat William IV" and the "Schooner(s) Ellen, Wood Duck, and Princess Victoria." Various commodities are charged appropriately: "Fruit and Oysters-2p;" "Whiskey, Ale, Fish, Lard, Salt per Barrel- 4p;" and so on. While most of the shipping was to and from Toronto, other ports, such as Prescott, Grimsby, Oswego and Ogdensburg, made Niagara-on-the-Lake an active international port in the late 1830s.

(969.50.1) **by Robert F. Kamm**

Robert Addison's Desk

The desk, circa 1800, is a handsome yet serviceable piece of furniture carved from black walnut. It would have been a notable feature in Addison's study, in constant use for the preparation of sermons and correspondence. The roomy interior reveals several pigeonholes for storing documents and letters, some of which surely must have come from the Society for the Propagation of the Gospel – a missionary organization based in England, where Addison was born. No secret compartments or repository of private documents have been discovered, but there are two drawers on each side with finely crafted dovetailed joints, evidence of good craftsmanship. It is not difficult to visualize the reverend gentleman working at his desk, illuminated by the light of wax candles, writing Sunday sermons or updating parish records for the parishioners of St. Mark's church. At the time of his arrival in Niagara 1792, there were more Presbyterians than adherents of the Church of England.

Thus when a call went out for the services of a priest, Addison responded, making the long voyage and bringing with him a valuable collection of books which now reside in the church library named in his honour, Addison Hall.

It can be said of him that he was a true missionary priest, ready to deal with the rigours of the Niagara frontier. (970.565) **by Jean M. Baker**

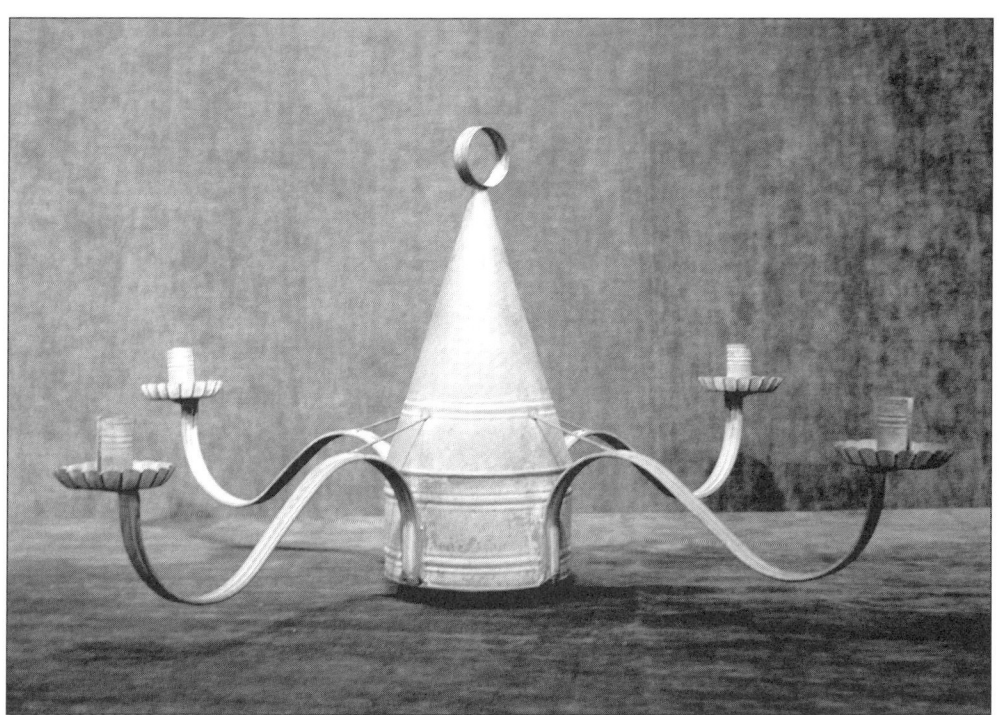

Tin Chandeliers

Although we take artificial light for granted today, this was not the case in the second quarter of the nineteenth century. In Niagara, the preferred illumination was the candle; however, candles were expensive to purchase and painstaking to make (either by dipping, or using a candle mold) and, as such, were sparingly used. Furthermore the illumination from a tallow (fat) candle was hardly any illumination at all. Chandeliers were only found in important buildings of the day, notably churches such as the Niagara-on-the-Lake Methodist Church, built in 1825, and the odd tavern, ballroom or theatre. Tin, by its very nature, was not particularly durable, but was a relatively economical and easily available material when compared to brass or pewter. Tinware was generally fabricated to order by local tinsmiths. It is almost certain that these elegant, well-designed chandeliers were fabricated in the Town of Niagara-on-the-Lake, in order to allow the church building to be used after dark. Museum research has attributed their likely fabrication to Richard Wagstaffe, a prominent Niagara tinsmith of the period. (970.581.1 & 970.581.2)

by Ken Douglas

Mechanics Institute Stove

A black cast iron stove, decorated in high relief, represents a significant technological advance of the nineteenth century.

It came from the Niagara Mechanics Institute, organized "to follow scientific pursuits and establish a library." Dr. John Whitelaw (1776-1855), one of its organizers, was a specialist in science and mathematics and the classics. It may have been used in his home at 307 Mississauga Street, built in 1818, where he taught school from 1833 to 1851. Before the advent of stoves, the common method of heating was the fireplace, indicated by the back to back fireplace in this house, and the one used for cooking in the basement.

Quantity production of cast iron stoves in North America began about 1828 and the first were of German design. Sizes and shapes multiplied, simulating the architecture of castles, churches and villas, creating some of the finest examples of casting known.

The precise date on which this stove was made is uncertain but its design was patented in 1855 by the builders of this stove, Vose & Company of Albany, New York, USA. Its length, width and height measure 48.8 x 53.3 x 39.4 cm. Its two hinged front doors are about 10 x 10 cm with a door of the same size in its right side. The opening to a chimney is in the back and the fuel used was wood.

This stove was used for heating but after the mid nineteenth century new designs incorporated an oven for cooking and fireplaces became mainly ornamental. (970.659(A&B))

by Cliff James

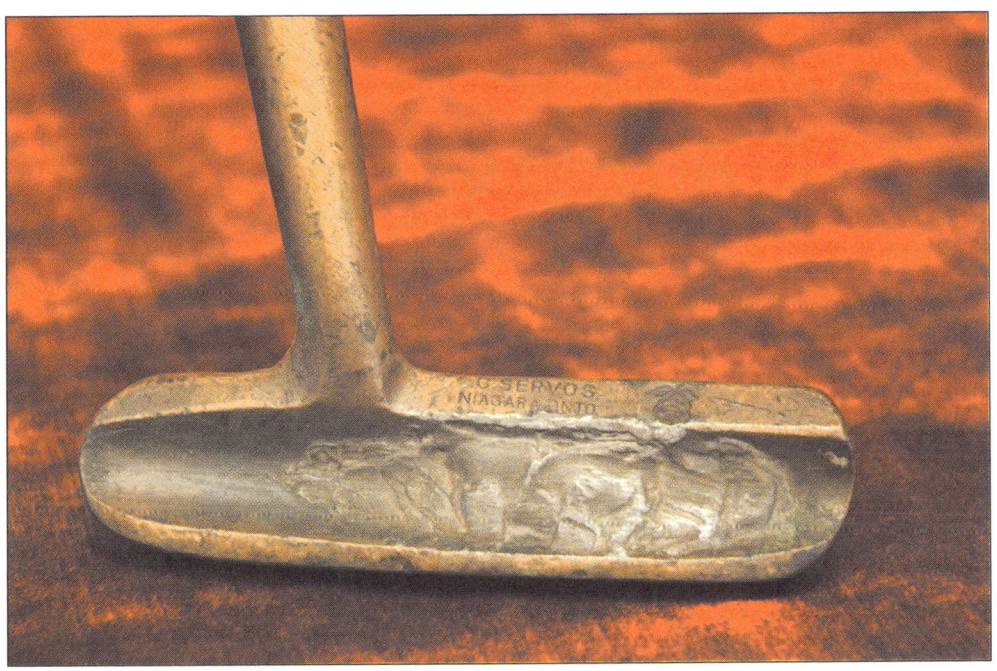

Putter engraved "L.C. Servos, Niagara Ont."

My first recollection of Lancelot Cressy Servos is when he would visit his mother, who lived in Niagara-on-the-Lake just across the street from my residence. Although he did not live in Niagara he did visit quite often. On several occasions I would see him going to the golf course with a couple of clubs and some golf balls. I would follow him and watch him hit good shots to the green, hoping some day I would be able to hit golf balls as well as he did. I was only in my early teens at the time.

Although there is no evidence of him ever having been a member of the Royal Niagara Golf Club, as it was known at that time, he was associated with the Club and in the early 1900s donated the Servos Trophy for competition by the men. This trophy is still being awarded.

Although he was a Canadian, most of his work concerning golf took place in the United States, mostly in Florida. He designed several of the oldest courses and, as stated in his book, which is reputed to be the first book on golf written in Canada, he would visit there, join up with other golf professionals and play a round. He says the merchants at that time would close their shops and go out to watch these professional golfers play.

Mr. Servos begins his book with this comment: "Time marches on. Man conspires, respires, aspires, and expires. During which sojourn, if he is fortunate, he plays a little golf and perspires. He may get so that he plays it very well. Or he may not be able to play it as well as he would like. It is for those who would like to improve their golf that this book is published. For what gaineth a man if he acquire the whole world and yet is unable to play golf?" (2004.007.007C)

by Al Derbyshire

Dolman Jacket Circa 1880
Label: Madame Rosalie Court Dress and Mantle Maker
176 Regent Street London

This lovely 1880s mantle, known as a dolman, was made in England from a mid nineteenth century hand-embroidered Kashmir shawl. These luxurious shawls, hand-woven in India since the late eighteenth century, were later known as Paislies when shawl manufacture was established by less costly methods in Scotland. Hand embroidery, done mostly in India, also made these much desired accessories more affordable.

The craze for these shawls reached its zenith with the voluminous skirts of the 1850s and 60s and declined with the bustle fashions of the 1870s. They were often made into garments contoured to fit over the new silhouette.

This dolman, so named because the cape-like sleeves are cut in one with the body, is made from red twill-weave wool, worked in multi-coloured woollen, silk and metallic threads. It is lined with a lambswool backed cream-coloured quilted silk satin.

The curvilinear shapes in different colours are appliquéd onto the red ground almost like a crazy quilt with very fine blanket and chain stitches.

The plastron-shaped front and back panels are in rich, dark blue silk velvet, decorated with coiled multi-coloured metallic braid in the manner of a Hussar's jacket, fastening down the front with hooks and eyes.

The pointed shape of the Paisley portion is made from the harlequin borders of a square shawl.

Exquisite polychrome silk fringe finished with small, covered wooden balls trims the sleeves and outer edges, sadly missing around the hem.

The garment was purchased by Mr. Charles Edward Verral of Toronto for his wife Charlotte Ann on a trip to London after their marriage in 1873. Perhaps Mrs. Verral wore her dolman on a visit to Niagara-on-the-Lake. (986.12)   **by Rita Brown**

House of Worth Walking Dress circa 1885

The fashion house founded in Paris in 1857 by Charles Frederick Worth is arguably the most influential and well known of the second half of the nineteenth century. For two generations, until the end of the Second World War, monarchs, rich titled courtiers, fashion forward socialites and aspiring socialites flocked to be dressed by these icons of fashion. This lovely copper and black silk satin walking dress dates from the mid 1880s and is a typical example of the Worth style: perfectly tailored with bold and impeccably chosen fabrics. The bodice includes a very small sailor style collar with a crossed necktie and lace at the neck. The sleeves, which have been designed with the stripe running up and down, have ruching and lace at the wrist. The skirt which would have been worn with a bustle as the undergarment has ties on the inside to gather the skirt up to a suitable length for walking.

The allure of a Worth gown cannot be underestimated. Even a walking dress such as this one would have been very costly and the cachet of wearing this dress while strolling the boulevard would have unmistakably set the wearer apart. "Indeed, the woman who was drawn to Worth not only wore showpieces but, in accordance with the feminine ideal of her time, was something of a showpiece herself." (Coleman, 1989)

While unfortunately we may never know the woman who wore this dress, she would have cut a lovely figure on the streets of late nineteenth century Niagara. (972.62)

by Kathy Powell

Niagara Falls Screen

Jean Zuber, a wallpaper manufacturer located in Rixheim, Alsace, France, commissioned Jean Julien Deltil, a French artist who had spent several years in America, to design a cycloramic scene of America. Zuber and Deltil were guided by the writings of the French naturalist Jacques Gerard Milbert, who had astutely observed American culture. The result of this collaboration, "Views of North America," first printed in 1834, is a masterpiece and its thirty-two breadths feature Niagara Falls as one of its scenes.

"Views of North America" presented an allegorical perception of Jacksonian America. The virtues of the republic were presented in vignettes that portrayed a romanticized vision of democracy. "The American Experiment" engaged foreign scrutiny. Concurrently an era of dissention was fomenting in British North America, aimed at achieving greater social equality and political representation.

The Historical Society's screen is a modified copy of the Zuber Niagara Falls image. It appears to be hand-painted and may be a unique interpretation of the Zuber scene produced in a decorator's studio or executed by an itinerant artist shortly after wallpaper first appeared. Alterations to Deltil's design, particularly the addition of a female riding side-saddle on her bounding horse, may have been requested by a client who commissioned the screen.

Although neither the steamship nor the train (altered into an omnibus in the painted copy), were present at Niagara Falls when "Views of America" was issued, the Niagara-on-the-Lake dock area was becoming a significant manufacturing site for these symbols of modernity. (1998.001.001)

by Peter Babcock

Library Box

When the Niagara Public Library was being renovated in the 1970s the librarians cleared out a large number of books. Heaps of old leatherbound books were placed on the floor, free for the taking. Among the books was a small, plain old box, about 36cm long by 13.5cm wide by 12cm high, the check out tray for the library. I took it home on principle, and subsequently donated it to the museum.

In those pre-computer days each book had a pocket with a card at the back. When the book was being checked out the borrower's name was written on the card and filed in the check out box under the due date. As a young person I found the check out process daunting. The librarian of the day managed to convey disappointment if she regarded the choice of book unsuitable, especially after my graduation from the children's to the adults' section at age twelve. It was always a relief to see the card filed and the transaction complete.

This box is a favourite of mine because it is a part of my own past experience. It feels personal. More than that, together with a cluster of related artefacts – small leatherbound volumes from the library and a newspaper clipping showing Miss Duddy (the Librarian) standing at the circulation desk beside this very box – it tells a story of a ritual now much changed and streamlined.

I do not know the date of the box itself, but regardless of date it is important because it was part of a place that goes back to the very beginning of the town.   (2005.011.015)

by Sandra Woodruff

Grape Press

This wine press is known as a "basket press". The classic icon of winemaking, it is a hand powered mechanical advantage system that moves the piston down a central screw.

The basket press may well have been the inspiration for Johannes Guttenberg, who came from a winegrowing region in Germany, to invent the printing press around 1440.

Pressing is done to separate the skins, seeds, and any other non-juice matter (the must) from the juice of the freshly picked grapes. There are several different types of presses used in the winery industry, including basket presses like this one built by Edward Ziraldo and Fred Ziraldo (uncle and father of Donald Ziraldo, respectively) at the Port Weller Dry Docks in the early 1950s.

The basket press is the most common historically because it produces clean, low-solids juice. The basket press has a screw and plate that compresses the must against the bottom and the basket slats and pushes the fruit down in a cylinder extracting the precious juice.

This press was used by Donald Ziraldo and Karl Kaiser to make their first table wines, in 1974, which were submitted to the Liquor Control Board of Ontario. These wines led to the issuance of the first winery license since Prohibition in 1929, to Inniskillin Wines in 1975.

Ironically many of the presses used in modern day wine making are pneumatic presses. However, because of their flexibility and strength the basket presses have once again become the predominant presses used in the making of Icewine – Canada's classic icon in winemaking. (2006.021.001) **by Donald Ziraldo**

Wampum

Wampum beads were manufactured by the Haudenosaunee (Iroquois) people through a difficult and painstaking process in which small, smooth, cylindrical beads were created out of shell. The word "wampum" is derived from the Algonkian word "wampumpeag." The beads vary in colour, from white to a dark purple-black, and each colour had a certain value attached to it, with the darker colours being more valuable. Along with the Haudenosaunee, other nations, largely those along the Northern Atlantic coast, manufactured and used wampum. Contrary to popular belief, wampum was not used by the Haudenosaunee as a direct form of currency, but rather as a means of exchange or barter. The beads had many other varied uses, including as a gift, given upon the negotiation of treaties, as a burnt offering upon the death of an individual, as an invitation to council, or even given to the family of a murder victim, as a compensation for the slaying. Wampum belts, which consist of many beads of varying colour strung together to form often complex patterns, were an important diplomatic tool among native peoples and acted like modern day treaties. Perhaps the best known of these belts is entitled The Hiawatha Belt, which memorializes the Iroquois Great Law of Peace uniting the original five nations, which were later joined by the sixth, the Tuscaroras. The Great Law represents one of the earliest forms of diplomacy, and has lasted far beyond modern treaties and alliances. Wampum belts, in various patterns, were also used to seal agreements with Europeans, including the Jesuits and the Vatican.   (970.143)

by Meredith Leonard

Archangel Gabriel Weathervane

The Fallen Angel of St. Andrew's is an interesting piece of Niagara's history. Made of sheet metal and coated in gold paint, it measures 7 feet 5 inches by 2 feet with a centre bulge to accommodate the pole. It depicts an angel in flight blowing his horn. This was the weathervane of St. Andrew's Presbyterian Church when it was reconstructed in 1831. The original church, completed in September 1795, was destroyed by fire on August 24, 1813 by American forces. They were retreating from the town during the conflict with the British.

Construction of the present St. Andrew's Church commenced on May 31, 1831 and was completed the same year. The church was crowned with this weathervane representing the Archangel Gabriel, where it remained for the next 24 years. Unfortunately, on April 18, 1855 at 6:45am, a "fearful hurricane" struck the town. The roof and gallery of St. Andrew's were severely damaged and the weathervane was blown from its lofty position. It was later found in a farmer's field and then lay in a barn for over 40 years before being donated to the Niagara Museum.

On close inspection of the weathervane one can see that it is bent, tarnished and cracked in places. These scars are an indication of the many indignities it has suffered. Despite this, like the church of St. Andrew's itself, the Archangel Gabriel Weathervane is a true survivor and a noteworthy part of Niagara's colourful history. (969.409)   **by Joan Hill**

Gorget

"The Gorget (Fr. gorge – a throat), that piece of armour which was worn round the neck, may be said to have been the last survival of plate armour used in the equipment of the British Army, with the exception of the cuirass, or breast and back plates, of the Household Cavalry." By 1684, the gorget was worn only by officers and had become a badge of rank worn only when on duty. From 1743, gorgets were either gilt or silver, according as the lace (and buttons) of the uniform were either gold or silver, but like this "Universal Pattern" gorget, they were gilt only after 1795. It was worn hung to the lower buttons of the collar of the coat, by loops of half-inch wide ribbon five inches long, with a tuft or rosette (both of the uniform facings colour) attached to the ribbons at the shoulders of the gorget. Gorgets were abolished by General Order No. 492, dated 2nd August, 1830. (971.204)

by Lt. Col. Bernard L. Nehring

Coatee of Lieutenant Daniel McDougal, Upper Canada Incorporated Militia Battalion, circa 1813-1814

This humble garment was once worn by a distinguished veteran officer who settled in Niagara-on-the-Lake. Daniel McDougal was born in Inverness, Scotland, in 1782 and came to Canada with his parents who settled in Glengarry County. When the war broke out in June 1812, he was in the Glengarry Militia and took part in the capture of Ogdensburg on 22 February 1813. On 20 March he obtained an ensign's commission in the Battalion of Upper Canada Incorporated Militia. He was promoted to the rank of lieutenant on 30 March and is said to have been at Fort George on 27 May when it was taken by the Americans, and later at Twelve Mile Creek. He was severely wounded at Lundy's Lane on 24 July 1814. Lying in the field after having been struck seven times, he was initially reported to be "mortally wounded." Although he recovered, McDougal had subsequent health problems as well as a lead ball in his body for the rest of his days. He nevertheless lived a long and active life.

McDougal's coatee respects Governor Simcoe's 1794 instructions, that is: scarlet with blue "facings" (i.e. the collar, cuffs and lapels) trimmed with "plain gilt metal buttons." To denote his lieutenant's rank, Daniel McDougal wore a gold epaulette with thin gold fringes on the right shoulder only. On 1 June1814, a gold lace edging was ordered added to cuffs and collars on the officers' coatees of the Upper Canada Militia. Thus Lieutenant McDougal's coatee was most likely made locally between the date of his first commission, in March 1813 and before the summer of 1814. Since they were in the field at the time, adding gold edging lace at the collar and cuffs was not an urgent matter for many officers and Lieutenant McDougal's coatee remained plain. The cuffs, quite small and without buttons, are the only exception to this otherwise regulation coatee.

When the coatee, now in possession of the museum, was donated a century ago, it was said to be the one that Lieutenant McDougal wore when he was wounded during the Battle of Lundy's Lane. McDougal was in no condition to resume his duties for many months. He was granted a small pension on account of his many wounds. So the coatee, apart from its cuffs, remained much the same as when he wore it in the field.

Garments with such a history are rare, even more so if made in Canada, and are fitting reminders of the sacrifices made by our forebears to keep our country free. (972.902)

by René Chartrand

Native Doll

Native children had few toys. Generally Native families had only what was essential for their daily lives. Hence games were most popular as they could simply be played with materials found at the sites. What toys they had were made of locally available material and expendable. Indigenous dolls were most often made of cattails, cornstalks and other natural materials found locally.

The fact that there are painted features on this doll is notable. Most native dolls were faceless, as it was feared the doll would turn into the person it represented if too much detail was on the doll. The doll is dressed in the ordinary costume of a Six Nations woman. She is made of wood and papier-mâché.

The materials are of European influence. Before the introduction of glass beads this native doll would have been decorated with bone, shell and stone beads. The clothing is black with a red sash and pants with blue stitching. The hair and eyes are painted brown and the skin pink. The date of this doll is estimated to be in the mid to late eighteen hundreds. This doll belonged to a Chief's daughter on the Grand River and was indeed very much cherished, as she is in excellent condition. The doll does not seem to have been ravaged by child's play, but rather admired and carefully handled by her owner. She was and is a treasure. (972.9)

by Alice Duc Trino

Dragoon Helmet of Sergeant Major Flanigan

The Niagara Historical Museum is home to a diverse display of historical artefacts. Among those artefacts visitors will see a handsome brass helmet. Engraved on the helmet one can read the following words: "1st OR The Kings Dragoon Guards".

In May, 1939, a ceremony was held at Fort Niagara to commemorate the Rush-Bagot Treaty, originally signed between Britain and the United States in 1817. This Treaty put a limitation on the guns aboard the Great Lakes vessels.

For this ceremony I was asked to take the role of Britannia. Britannia is always portrayed wearing a helmet. My American counterpart represented the District of Columbia. Mr. George Wilkinson represented Britain's Secretary of State (Bagot). We stood on a raised dais where flags and coloured draperies floated in the stiff breeze. Directly below, the land dropped away into the white-capped lake. I especially recall the brilliance of the sun and the glorious effect it had on the polished surface of the helmet. When I wore it, I felt like Britannia.

There was a poignancy to this occasion, for war clouds were gathering and those present had mixed feelings of unity, mutual support and foreboding. (972.917.1) **by Kaye Toye**

1790s Tea Set

"Will you come for tea?" This invitation was often extended to ladies in Niagara during the earliest years of the settlement.

The tradition of drinking tea was carried on from its beginnings in Britain in the mid seventeenth century. Originally, due to the extremely high cost of tea, it had been enjoyed primarily by the upper classes.

On arrival in North America, ladies of the aristocratic or noble classes proudly continued with their customs. Lieutenant-Governor John Graves Simcoe wanted to recreate Britain here, to restore the prestige that had been lost in the colonies. He stated that "the utmost attention should be paid that British Customs, Manners and Principles in the most trivial as well as serious matters should be promoted."

The rituals of afternoon tea, dinner parties and dances are recorded as frequent events in Elizabeth Simcoe's diary. Her own set of china, which had arrived from England, had been unpacked and placed in the temporary kitchen (an arbour of oak boughs). Within hours, the dishes were removed, as the arbour was on fire and unfortunately, almost all were broken.

This tea set of soft paste porcelain is typical of the period and was, undoubtedly, used for the enjoyment of the ladies of Newark. (988.122.1)

by Ann Lindsay

RJR Tile of Evans Cottage

In the early 1960s , a newly married couple who lived in Toronto discovered Niagara-on-the-Lake. They both led very busy lives in Toronto and decided a country house would provide a perfect retreat from a hectic city life.

There was only one real estate agent in town at that time and it took him two years to find a house that was affordable. It was being sold by Mrs. Esme Allen and was located at 36 Picton Street. The house was called "the Evans Cottage." It was built around 1832 and needed renovations. Esme, who lived nearby, would drop in from time to time to see the improvements that were being made to the house.

On one of these visits she presented the new owners with a contemporary tile that portrayed the house. It was nicely glazed and was 7 inches wide by 8 inches high. The drawing of the house was naive but there was no doubt it was the Evans Cottage. The back had been scooped out to prevent warping in the kiln. The tile had been made locally at the RJR Shop and Kiln that was located in a small cottage on the property of Dr. Bruce Rigg, a local general practitioner.

The owners of the Evans Cottage were thrilled. In spite of two cracks on the surface of the tile, it was immediately given pride of place on the living room mantle. There it remained until the house was sold. (988.158.2) **by Joan Draper**

Portrait of Lt. Col. John Butler (1728-1796)

This portrait of Lt. Col. John Butler, oil on wood panel, 15 by 19 inches, was copied from the original by Henry Oakley in 1834, and donated to the Niagara Historical Society by Miss Oakley of Bronte, Ontario.

Butler was born in Connecticut, brought up on the American frontier, joined the British army and led Butler's Rangers and troops of Natives during the American Revolution. Later he was stationed in Fort Niagara. He later founded a new settlement across the Niagara River, Niagara-on-the-Lake. Here he lived, farmed, governed and died.

There are five versions of Butler's portrait known to exist, described below. They are all right-side facing profiles, his hair long and curling – same man, same pose and uniform. There are differences in expression, in the epaulet, in size and technique.

Known portraits of Lt. Col. John Butler:

1. An amateur engraved mezzotint, possibly drawn from a likeness of Colonel Butler taken during his lifetime. Part of the official papers of General Frederick Haldimand (1718-1791). Held in the library of the British Museum.
2. A photographic reproduction of the above print "The only authentic image available in Canada of Col. Butler." This belongs to the Library and Archives, Canada (LAC).
3. A watercolour, a nineteenth century copy after the above print at LAC.
4. A book illustration of "Indian Leaders in the War of the Revolution" in *Picture Gallery of Canadian History* by C.W. Jefferys, 1942, Vol. 1.
5. Niagara Historical Society Museum portrait. An unofficial military portrait, rather bold, unrefined, charming and in colour. (988.194)

by Percy Webb

William Dickson by Hoppner Meyer

The small watercolour portrait of the late Honourable William Dickson is the work of the late artist Hoppner Francis Meyer. William Dickson emigrated from Scotland in 1784 in his teens to work for his cousin, prominent Niagara merchant Robert Hamilton. From his own early success as a local businessman, Dickson went on to become a well-respected lawyer and politician. As a land speculator, Dickson gained notoriety for his purchase, in 1811, and the subsequent development of "Block 1" of the Haldimand Tract (along the Grand River). Through his encouragement and help in the placement of emigrant Scottish settlers between 1826 and 1835, William Dickson is fondly regarded as the founder of Galt and the Township of Dumfries.

Like Dickson, British-born portrait artist Hoppner Francis Meyer emigrated to Canada as a young man in 1832. The son of a well-known German painter, Hoppner Meyer was named after his father's friend, successful English portrait painter John Hoppner. By 1861, he and his family had moved to St. Catharines from Toronto, eventually returning to England near the end of his life. He is noted for his 8 x 10 inch watercolour portraits of such prominent men as Sir John Beverley Robinson and the Hon. Robert Baldwin. Author William Colgate's description of Meyer's painting style as being marked by "a simple directness and charm" is certainly noticeable in the small portrait of an aging William Dickson, dated 1842. Dickson died only four years later, in his 77th year, at his stately home "Woodlawn" in Niagara. The Dickson house, still standing on John Street in Niagara-on-the-Lake, was later enlarged and renamed "Randwood." (988.199)   **by Sherry Spark**

View of Fort Niagara by John Herbert Caddy

An important early watercolour in the Niagara Historical Society and Museum is entitled "View of Fort Niagara" by Anglo-Canadian artist John Herbert Caddy (1801-1883). Born to a military family posted at Quebec City, Caddy enrolled as a cadet at the Royal Military College in Woolich, England in 1816 where he learned to paint and draw topographical views for military use. Commissioned in 1825, he served in the West Indies (1828-1831, 1833-1837), British Honduras (1838-1841) and London, Canada West (1842-1844). Ample leisure time at these postings enabled him to develop his painting and other interests. A surveyor and engineer in London after his retirement, in 1861 Caddy moved to Hamilton where success as a teacher and artist enabled him to devote himself entirely to his painting, primarily landscapes.

Although the painting was in the Collection prior to 1972, information about the watercolour is slim. A view of Fort Niagara across the Niagara River from approximately the corner of Front and King Streets, its precision suggests Caddy may have used mechanical aids in its creation; Caddy's style was usually less structured. We know he came to the Niagara region several times (undocumented) after he moved to Hamilton. Was it painted prior to 1833 as the inscription states or later, after he settled in Hamilton, as is more likely? Its size suggests that it may have been painted in the studio from on-the-spot studies. Ultimately we know that Caddy's creation offers an exceptional panoramic view of an important town feature in about the middle of the nineteenth century.

(988.228)

by Gary Essar

Sampler by Augusta Stewart

Fragile and ephemeral, cross-stitch samplers are among the few surviving artefacts of the domestic lives of young girls and women of the fifteenth to nineteenth centuries. As tangible evidence of their daily work, samplers offer a rare glimpse into the concerns and pursuits of our feminine ancestors. Unfortunately, their fragility and sensitivity to light also means they are seldom on display. The Niagara Historical Society has exhibited the samplers from its collection only three times in the past two decades.

This charming and well-balanced sampler, completed by Augusta Stewart at Niagara in March 1834, is one of 29 samplers in the Niagara Historical Society's permanent collection. It is stitched entirely in cross and Algerian eye stitches; its colours of muted green, tan and gold silk are most likely faded from their original, more vivid hues. Bounded with a regular green and gold border, it features three alphabets, two sets of numerals and ten decorative horizontal bands – some stitched over two threads of linen and some over one. There are two spot motifs: a fruit basket (symbol of fertility) and two evergreen trees (symbols of life). It is damaged in five places.

Little is known about Augusta Stewart – her age, her family, whether she remained in Niagara or whether she had any descendants. The most charming thing about her sampler is the inclusion of two opening verses of the Isaac Watts poem praising the industriousness of bees. "How skillfully she builds her cell," stitched young Augusta in her careful way – neatly demonstrating a prized nineteenth century feminine virtue. (901.112)

by Marlene Bergsma

Servos Cup

Amongst the artefacts at the Niagara Historical Museum are many items which have little or no provenance. One such item is a "horn cup" which once belonged to the Servos family. On close examination this beaker proved to be of turned wood, well polished to emulate horn, with an inset wood base. It is lined with sterling silver, the rim bearing a scalloped pattern. This rim bears hallmarks which indicate that it was manufactured by the firm of George Ashforth and Company of Sheffield, England between 1773 and 1783.

The origin of the cup and where and how the silver lining was added is a mystery. Ashforth was mainly known for the manufacture of such items as tea and coffee pots, candlesticks and salt cellars; so it is strange to find a beaker lined with their silver. One conjecture might be that the lining was part of a flat silver piece, while the rim was adapted from a small item such as a salt cellar. Who knows?

Since the Loyalist Servos brothers came to Niagara from Schoharie, New York in 1778, it may be assumed that the cup came into their possession after the American Revolution. Whether it was before they moved to Ontario is unknown. It is purported to have belonged to Jacob Servos who settled north of the present Lakeshore Road. (FA69.3.42)

by Jean & Les Taylor

Isaac Brock's Hat
(972.275.2)   by Ed Werner

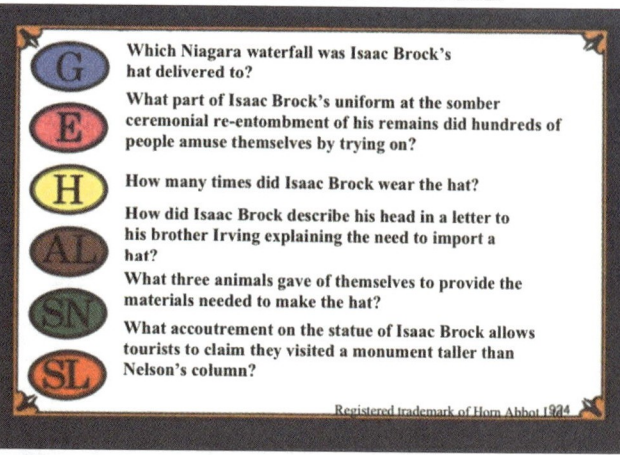

- **G** — Which Niagara waterfall was Isaac Brock's hat delivered to?
- **E** — What part of Isaac Brock's uniform at the somber ceremonial re-entombment of his remains did hundreds of people amuse themselves by trying on?
- **H** — How many times did Isaac Brock wear the hat?
- **AL** — How did Isaac Brock describe his head in a letter to his brother Irving explaining the need to import a hat?
- **SN** — What three animals gave of themselves to provide the materials needed to make the hat?
- **SL** — What accoutrement on the statue of Isaac Brock allows tourists to claim they visited a monument taller than Nelson's column?

Registered trademark of Horn Abbot Ltd.

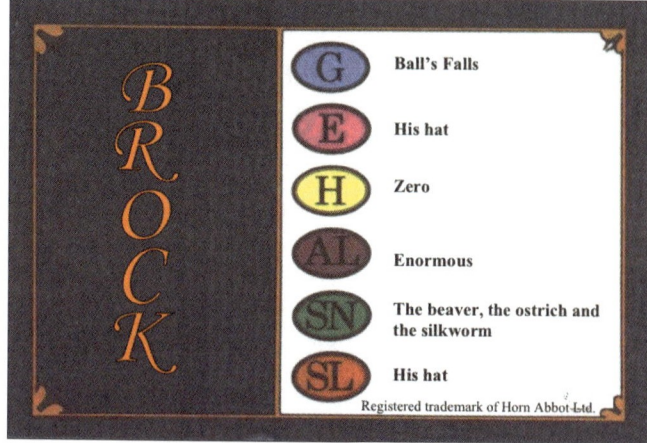

BROCK

- **G** — Ball's Falls
- **E** — His hat
- **H** — Zero
- **AL** — Enormous
- **SN** — The beaver, the ostrich and the silkworm
- **SL** — His hat

Registered trademark of Horn Abbot Ltd.

"Janet Carnochan" by E. Wyly Grier

To mark its 25th anniversary in 1921 the Niagara Historical Society commissioned this portrait of its founder, Miss Janet Carnochan, by the foremost Canadian portraitist E. Wyly Grier of Toronto. The $1000.00 fee was raised entirely through donations collected over a two-year period – some as small as one dollar. A letter seeking contributions for Miss Carnochan's portrait states: "From the day of its inception in December, 1895, she has uninterruptedly filled the presidential chair. In fact, no meeting of the society… has been presided over by any other officer or member during the entire period of the Society's existence. … A quarter of a century is a long time in which to continuously hold office in a society whose officers are annually elected."

The formal, life-size portrait is intended to convey Janet Carnochan's status and prominence. More than a mere likeness, it suggests contradictory traits of charm and strength of character, sternness and accessibility. The traditional setting, forward facing no-nonsense pose, delicate lace trim on the dress and the elaborate gilt frame add to the commanding presence of the portrait.

Janet Carnochan was born in 1839 in Starmford, Ontario. Despite her life-long commitment to numerous educational, community and church activities she is best remembered for her role as founder and ardent supporter of the Niagara Historical Society, having donated the land for the building which became the Museum, and presided over the acquisition of 10,000 articles for the collection. Accounts indicate she was "indefatigable in her organizing, collecting for, compiling information of, and writing pamphlets on the history of this town and district." When she died on April 1st, 1926, she was at her home next door to the Museum.

Artist E. Wyly Grier was born in Melbourne, Australia in 1862 and studied art in London, Rome and Paris. His 1895 marriage to Miss Dickson, an accomplished pianist from Niagara-on-the-Lake, introduced him to the town and its history. By the time Janet Carnochan sat for her portrait his work was well known in Canada and England. Some years later, in 1935, he was knighted by King George V for his outstanding services to Canadian arts and letters. (988.246)

by Sandra Lawrence

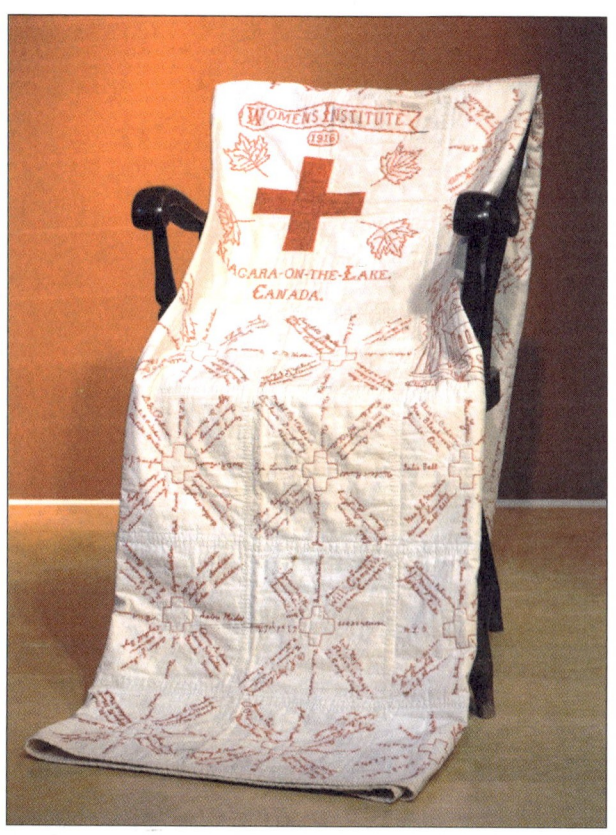

WWI Women's Institute Quilt

An autograph quilt was one of many articles for fundraisers carried out by the Women's Institute of Niagara during the "Great War." Completed in 1917, the quilt raised $150 for the Red Cross. Cotton squares measuring approximately 8 inches square were sold for $16 and a maximum of 16 people signed their names on each one. Then the Women's Institute members sewed over the autographs in red thread as well as outlining memorable buildings of the town. There are 80 squares on the quilt of which 69 have signatures.

The centre square has a large red cross surrounded by maple leaves. Buildings depicted include Fort Mississauga, the Museum, and each of the churches (St. Andrew's, St. Mark's, St. Vincent de Paul, and Methodist – today's Grace United Church) accompanied by the pastor's signature. Among notable squares is Janet Carnochan's where her titles of vice-president of the Ontario Historical Society and president of Niagara's society are recorded, and that of Nenagh Hall on Queen Street which today is known as the Charles Inn. Several military units paid for squares.

Following World War I, the autograph quilt was put on display in the Historical Museum. Just as visitors did 80 and more years ago, I enjoy reading the signatures and noting names that are familiar: Secord, MacLachlan, Watson, White, McNulty, Lansing, Dick, Armstrong, Mitchell, Campbell, Allen, Patterson, Currie, Elizabeth Ascher (who helped the Polish soldiers training at Niagara the next year), Dr. Anderson, Flynn, Hiscott, Rigg, Wigmore, Waugh, Woodruff, Lee, Wright, Phillips, Wooton, Gordon, Duff, Ball, Doyle, Rand, McFarland, Servos. Have a look and see if you recognize others. (972.263)

by Elizabeth Masson

Uniform of Fort-Major Donald Campbell

This coat is a very early type, common shortly after 1800. It features blue facings, buttons in pairs, a rounded cut at the waist and white piping. The high stand-up collar is missing. There is an epaulet at the left shoulder, but it isn't known whether this is original to the coat.

Being the Fort-Major of Fort George (an administrative position) meant you worked directly for the British army and did not report to any particular regiment. Your rank might not even be major. It was usually more junior.

As Fort-Major, Campbell could have worn a coat of one of his previous regiments. None of them, however, had blue facings and paired buttons. There is also the possibility that Campbell bought this coat from another officer. It does resemble the warrant for the 10th Royal Veterans Battalion, which was in Canada at that time. It is more likely that this coat was made for Campbell in a generic British officer's style. There appears to be no specific uniform requirement for his position.

Campbell had a long and wide-ranging career in the military. In his senior years, the position as Fort-Major would have been very welcome. His family lived with him in Niagara. Campbell died of unknown causes in December 1812, at age 57, and was buried in the central west bastion of Fort George.

Campbell's son tried to buy his father's burial plot many years later. It isn't known if the burial site was disturbed during reconstruction of Fort George during the 1930s.

The Campbell family suffered through the trials of war in Niagara. They lost a loved one, were caught in the middle of the Battle of Fort George (May 27, 1813), endured American occupation and were burned out, along with the rest of the town, on December 10, 1813.

(972.903) **by Glenn Smith**

Glass Walking Sticks

Among the more unusual items in the Museum, and perhaps the most stunning, is a collection of 24 glass walking sticks. Although completely impractical, thousands of glass canes were crafted in the glasshouses of England, Europe and the United States for over four centuries.

For the sheer delight of making lovely and interesting "objets," glassmakers would, on their own time, take the left-over sand, soda ash and lime of their trade and create pieces for their own use and pleasure or to improve their skills. They worked with molten glass to make glass chains, sock darners, bells, rolling pins, horns and walking sticks. These "Friggers" in England or "glasshouse whimsies" elsewhere were often given as gifts or used to decorate the houses of these master craftsmen.

There are two types of glass canes – the first was made out of a solid piece of twisted glass with spirals of coloured glass forming its core and decorated with a crook or handle. The second was made from blown glass and is hollow with a rounded knob handle. Some of these canes were as tall as five meters.

One of the first uses of these sticks was ceremonial – they were carried by glassmakers in their guild parades. Later, copying Marie Antionette's playing the rustic shepherdess at the Petit Trianon, fashionable English ladies carried glass shepherd's crooks decorated with flowers and ribbons. In the nineteenth century, glass canes were part of the costume of some English dandies.

The museum's collection of glass whimsies was the gift of the Toronto interior designer, David Whitmore, who owned a house on the corner of Victoria and Johnson Streets until his death in 1998. (1998.003.112 - 1998.003.135)   **by Virginia Mainprize**

Daguerreotype of Elizabeth Clench (nee Johnson)

Elizabeth Clench was the wife of Ralfe Clench, first magistrate of Upper Canada, the daughter of Margaret Campbell and Brant Johnson and granddaughter of Sir William Johnson and his second wife, a Mohawk.
Elizabeth was born in 1772 in Montgomery, New York. She was a United Empire Loyalist, listed in the Niagara census in 1783.

Shown in the picture is a travelling case approximately 3x3 inches in dark brown leather with grapes and maple leaves tooled into the leather. The daguerreotype oval picture is surrounded by gold tooled pebbled paper with red velvet surrounds. The opposite side of the case is a faded red/pink silk made to protect the picture when closed.

The picture shows a rather severe looking woman in her later years, with folded hands, white lace ruffles around her face in the form of a cap and white lace collar and cuffs on her pink and black dress. Elizabeth died in 1850, outliving her husband by 22 years.

Apparently Elizabeth kept a fine home for her husband and twelve children, entertaining many visiting dignitaries. The property, a whole block, was given to her husband in 1796. The house was built in approximately 1804, and survived the War of 1812 because the Clench family formed a bucket brigade the day of the Big Fire. According to some reports, either intentionally or not, the property was set on fire later by some Natives and displaced two families, the Clenches and Stewarts, leaving seventeen souls homeless.

Elizabeth's husband, besides occupying many political posts, was taken prisoner, helped start the Presbyterian Church, the Agricultural Society, Niagara Library and the Turf Club and joined the Masonic Lodge #19, involving Elizabeth and her entertaining abilities.

(992.089) **by Harriet "Sis" Bunting Weld**

John Swinton's Toolbox

John Swinton's toolbox, which dates from the early 1800s, appears to have a dual purpose. On one hand, this apparently plain wooden chest, painted black with rope handles at each end, was used as a container for his tools. On the other hand, and perhaps more importantly, as one examines the interior, it becomes obvious that this man used the box as an example of his craftsmanship. The owner's name is painted on the front and its condition is "fair – good".

The underside of the lid is made of mahogany-coloured wood, which is cleverly inlaid with a delicate diamond pattern. Inside the box, at the top, are two wooden trays lying lengthways along the back and along the front, with a space in the middle to provide access to several drawers. The trays contain a series of drawers with white knobs and may be moved from front to back on metal channels attached to the insides of the box. Underneath these top trays is another set of trays, again with drawers, and again one being in front and one at the back. Altogether, there are fourteen drawers in the back units, nine in the lower and five in the upper. As well, the top unit has a hinged lid to provide access to the top section. The front units have fifteen drawers, nine in the lower, four in the upper and two small drawers, which may be seen at the lower right when the bottom front unit is moved toward the back.

In the bottom of the box and in the centre cavity are several tools. These are as follows: two keyhole saws, one large-handled chisel device, one bow saw, two soldering irons, two squares, one axe, one wooden mallet, two two-handled shaving tools, one small claw hammer, one brass compass engraved with the date 1809 and the name, J. Robinson, one marking gauge, one large wooden plane and a set of ten routing planes, each with its own individual design for carving mouldings, cornices, etc. The large wooden plane and the set of routing planes are all hand-made, most likely by Swinton. All in all, this artefact and its contents demonstrate that John Swinton was a true craftsman. (969.104) **by Ed McCarthy**

Family Box

A utilitarian object of impeccable local provenance, superb craftsmanship in original condition – what more could one ask for?

This walnut box, 30 cm in height arrived at the Museum in 1980 as part of the Servos Collection transferred from Parks Canada, having been obtained from the last member of the Servos Family at Palatine Hill on the Four Mile Creek.

This late 17th – early 18th century box was designed to hold and conceal valuable papers/documents, perhaps a small Bible, coins, medals and jewellery, miniature family portraits and other treasured keepsakes – now long forgotten.

The square-domed lid of the box contains a secret compartment. Below, the front opens by a concealed peg, revealing 2 rows of small drawers, behind one of which is a smaller hidden compartment. The hand-forged iron lock and escutcheon plus hinges are fastened with early rose-headed nails.

The Servos family was living in the German Palatinate during the late 1600s, where it is thought the box originated. The patriarch of the North American family arrived in the Province of New York on the Charlotte River in 1726 with a letter of introduction, probably kept in the box.

During the American Revolution, four Servos brothers remained loyal to the Crown with two brothers, Captain Daniel and Lieutenant Jacob, serving with the British Indian Department. They and their families arrived at Niagara as refugees in the early 1780s with only a few possessions, including the box. Daniel operated grist and sawmills as well as a general store on the Four Mile Creek where he erected his home, Palatine Hill, the earliest surviving house in Niagara until it burned in 1950s. What an odyssey.

(FA69.3.194) **by Dr. Richard Merritt**

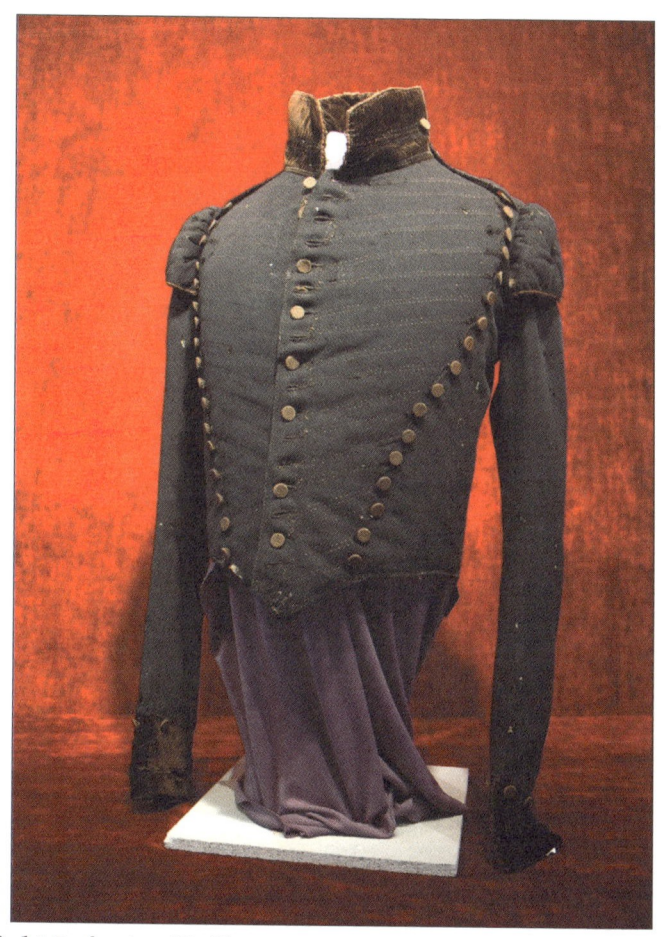

Glengarry Light Infantry Uniform

Raised in 1812, the Glengarry Light Infantry had a distinguished fighting record during the War of 1812. Its men were to be clothed originally in Highland garb but this was changed to a green uniform typical of a rifle regiment. The jacket was dark green with a high black collar, pointed cuffs with white piping and three vertical rows of buttons down the front. The trousers were green with black gaiters. Head gear was a black shako with green trim and black peak in front and was topped by a green plume. The collection includes a belt plate and a shako badge, missing the G of GLI. Other components of the uniform were a winter fur cap, a red sash that officers wore across the right shoulder, and black leather belts that supported a bayonet and an ammunition pouch. The two belts crossed in front and were held in place by the belt plate engraved with a Scottish thistle.

Despite its name, few of the regiment's men came from Glengarry County in Upper Canada. They were recruited from all parts of British North America (many had close ties to the Niagara region) and included men from the British Isles, continental Europe and the United States. The Glengarry Light Infantry fought using the skirmishing tactics of light infantry, and took part in several major battles in the Niagara Peninsula as well as raids into New York. Over 1400 men served in the regiment before it was disbanded in the summer of 1816. (972.910)

by Wesley Turner

Watercolour of The Chief Justice Robinson

In 2006, I donated some family items to the Niagara Historical Museum, including an 1850s watercolour of the paddle-wheeler *Chief Justice Robinson*, which my great-great-grandfather, Captain Duncan Milloy, sailed between Toronto, Niagara, and Lewiston in 1853-54. Subsequently I learned that the Museum owned another version of the image, created in 1904 when one of my ancestors allowed the original to be copied. The reproduction is faithful to the 1850s image, although it lacks the background details of the earlier picture and has the "feel" of the Edwardian period rather than the Victorian. Yet, it was fascinating to see how the Niagara Historical Society took an interest in documenting the *Robinson* a century ago.

The Niagara Harbour and Dock Company built the 315-ton *Chief Justice Robinson* in 1842. She was 23 broad x 167 feet long. One distinguishing feature was a plough-like bow for cutting through the ice in winter (and which Canada Post commemorated as part of a series of stamps on ice ships in 1978). The *Robinson* last served as a steamer in 1856; then was converted into a scow at the Shickluna shipyard. The vessel was named after Sir John Beverley Robinson, a veteran of the battle of Queenston Heights who held several high offices in pre-Confederation Ontario, including chief justice, a post he occupied from 1829 to 1862. The watercolour itself was the creation of Francis Hincks Granger, whose artworks included a number of views of Niagara in the mid 1850s, some of which are housed today in the excellent collection of the Toronto Reference Library.

I am glad that my original 1850s watercolour of the *Chief Justice Robinson* now finds a home at the Museum, and I trust that it (and the 1904 copy) will contribute to the interpretation of local history, marine heritage, and the story of the evolution of Ontario's museum collections. (988.203)

by Carl Benn

Two views of King Street by F.H. Granger

The first painting is entitled "A View from the Mouth of the Niagara River Towards the Foot of King Street, Niagara, C. W., 1854." Watercolour over pencil on paper (260 x 435 mm.), signed F. H. Granger.

The second is entitled "A View of Fort Niagara and the Mouth of the Niagara River from the Foot of King Street, Niagara C. W., 1854." Watercolour over pencil on paper (260 x 422 mm), unsigned.

Both watercolours were purchased from the artist by the Niagara Historical Society.

The artist, Francis Hincks Granger, was born in Surrey, England on July 29, 1829 and died in Niagara on April 6, 1906.

On attached labels for both views, dated 1856, and from other sources the buildings are identified as Fort Mississauga, a brick Martello tower built 1814-15, and the Gleaner Printing Office (middle) built in 1817 for the publication of the Gleaner and Niagara newspaper (1817-1837). Below is the residence of its proprietor and publisher, Andrew Heron, Sr. (1765–1848). The lowest building is the Oates Tavern, built about 1820. These buildings were demolished around 1866 for the site of the Queen's Royal Hotel. (1866-1931). The Guardhouse shown here was built in 1815 and moved to Butler's Barracks before 1866. The residence of Walter Elliot (1798–1858), an innkeeper, was built about 1835 and used as a tavern and boarding house by the family for three generations; the residence of John Dugdale (1810-1874), a soap and candle maker, was built about 1832. The Dugdale soap and candle factories, on the hill above, were built about 1850 and demolished or removed after 1854 for the Erie and Niagara Railway right-of-way. (988.189 & 988.195) **by Peter White**

Susan Chubbuck Sampler

This charming traditional sampler is the work of Susan Chubbuck, 1848. The Chubbucks were well known early merchants in Niagara. Job Chubbuck built the Chubbuck block, a large building on Front Street in Queenston, which was used at various times as a boarding house, restaurant, bank and hotel. It later became known as the Fisher block or Ivy block. Laura Chubbuck, daughter of Job, married Thomas McMicking. Their daughter, Laura Augusta, married Carl Fisher. The Fishers owned Dulverton farm, and their three sons built large houses along the Niagara Parkway between Lines 6 and 8. One of these, a graceful red brick Edwardian house owned by C. Howard Fisher, was built in 1907. There is a date stone in the basement, and the house boasts a large turret, wide verandah and enormous attic. Mrs. Carl Fisher's daughter-in-law, Grace, recounts that the attic was filled with old clothing, dresses and hats, all the accouterments of daily life and was a favourite place to play "dress-up." Howard Fisher sold the house to Henry and Erna Jahnke in 1965. It was in this high-ceilinged house with its lovely oak pocket doors, impressive wood bannister and wondrous attic, Henry and Erna's daughter, this author, acquired her love for all things old and antiquated, which she carries to this day. At an auction of the house contents prior to the sale, a box of assorted linens was purchased and in this box, the sampler stitched by Susan Chubbuck was found. Mrs. Jahnke donated this sampler to the Niagara Historical Museum in 1995. (994.484)

by Inge Saczkowski

Rural Matinee by Capt. John D. Shawe

For many youngsters in Niagara-on-the-Lake during the 1940s and 50s, Saturday afternoons were the highlight of the week. It was matinee movie time at the Brock Theatre. Shortly before 2:00 pm, my brother and I would join the line of excited kids on the street in front of the Brock. An edge of impatience could be felt as some of us engaged in a bit of friendly horse play, always with an eye on the clock in the marquee as it moved toward 2 o'clock. Finally, the doors would open and our fun began as we entered the world of movie marvels of that time.

In his painting entitled "Rural Matinee" (circa 1950) Captain John Shawe managed to capture the essence of that very special moment in the lives of children of the area. His use of warm, playful tones creates the core of his *oeuvre*. Soft lines help to fuse the figures with the surroundings in a harmonious fashion. These qualities contribute to a delightful and engaging composition.

Captain Shawe was a well known and respected figure in Niagara-on-the-Lake from the time he arrived in 1945. He and his wife, Marguerite, came to Niagara after World War II to retire from his life in the military. Not only had Captain Shawe served in the Armed Forces through two World Wars, but he had also been a circus stunt rider, an amateur yachtsman and an accomplished artist.

Thank you, Captain, for the marvellous memories your painting evokes. (2003.010.001)

by Vicky Tobe Wright

Pocketbook "Property of Martin McClellan, Niagara December 21, 1812"

It was May 26th, 1813; the wife of Captain Martin McClellan of the 1st Lincoln Militia left the family farm on John Street and found safety three miles away. Martin McClellan visited her in Virgil and provided his wife with his watch and this pocketbook. He told his wife that he would never see her or their children again.

For five days, McClellan had seen what the rest of the British garrison in Niagara could also see. Across the Niagara River, there were thousands of American troops on parade around Fort Niagara, workers preparing batteries and boats and 17 armed vessels returning triumphantly from the burning of York. McClellan and the small garrison in Niagara would be no match.

As fog lifted at daybreak the following day, McClellan saw 16 ships, 134 boats and scows (each with 30 to 50 American soldiers) two miles from the Town of Niagara. By 9 o'clock, some 2,300 American soldiers started the land assault under the cover of heavy artillery. The British defence was approximately 567 men, both regulars and militia. It took several attempts for the Americans to assemble on a plain at the western end of the town.

McClellan was in line with the rest of his company facing the U.S. forces a mere 5 to 10 meters away. The two sides fought for over 15 minutes. In the end, the British were forced to retreat, leaving 300 dead or wounded soldiers lying in the field. Martin McClellan was one of them. He died in defence of his country, his home and his family. (971.171.1B) **by Clark Bernat**

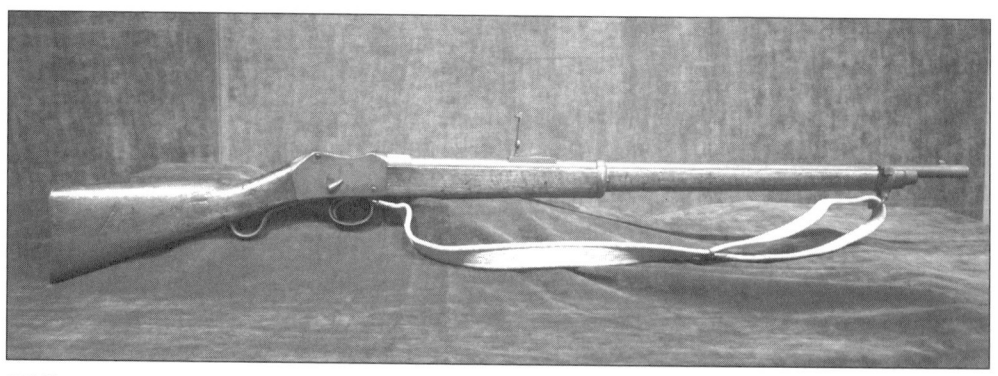

Rifle

This steel barreled, Italian walnut stocked Martini-Henry (Enfield) rifle was used by those Niagara militiamen who participated, under the command of Colonel Sir Frederick Middleton, in the suppression of the Northwest Rebellion of 1885. The rifle had been adopted by the British army and Canadian militia in 1871 and continued in service into the twentieth century. It was the first purpose-designed breech loading rifle in the British Army. It was a combination of the falling block mechanism devised by Frederich Martini (1832-97), a Swiss gunsmith, and the seven-groove rifling devised by Edinburgh gunsmith Alexander Henry (1817-95). The Martini-Henry was popular with the soldiers because it only weighed 9 lb (4 kg) unloaded, was very robust, easy to strip and clean, and had few and easily replaceable parts.

Frederick Middleton was born in Belfast, Ireland, in 1825 and saw service in many parts of the British Empire, including Quebec, where he had married Eugénie Doucet of Montreal. In 1884, he had accepted the normally placid position of General Officer commanding Canada's militia. As a consequence of his victory over the ill-equipped Métis rebels at the Battle of Batoche (in what is now Saskatchewan) on 12 May 1885, and the capture of their leader Louis Riel three days later, Middleton was granted a gift of $20,000 from the Parliament of Canada and given a knighthood by Queen Victoria. He resigned command of the Canadian Militia in 1890 and returned to Great Britain, where he was rewarded with the sinecure of Keeper of the Crown Jewels. He died in 1898.

(971.271) **by Neil Middleton**

Leather Tea Caddy: The Art of Tea Drinking

The rare art of tea drinking has been celebrated for centuries. Tea was such a valued commodity it was traded as we might trade petroleum today; the term "under lock and key" may be applied to give us an idea of how valued this consumable luxury was to our forbears. In a household of great means the master or mistress would hold a key to the tea caddy, as would a senior and trusted member of staff. The ceremony would begin with the caddy being opened to reveal a silver foil lined compartment or compartments, and in some cases a crystal mixing bowl. This bowl was used to blend the exotic teas. When the tealeaves had been well used, or simply spent, the "slop" would return to the pantry or kitchens, where it would be stretched by the lesser mortals of the household for a much weaker mug of tea.

It might be said that it is a rare thing to find a tea caddy made of such exotic and valued materials as tortoise shell, mother of pearl and abalone, fruitwoods, silver, silver-gilt, or even gold. Wouldn't it be even more rare to find an 18th or even 19th century tea caddy made of tooled leather? This early 19th century tooled leather caddy was once owned by a British army officer, Dr. Anderson Lowe. It is rare indeed that it has survived in relatively good condition, being of a material prone to disintegration over time. The cylindrical oval-shaped body with hinged cover and foiled interior has a small swing handle finial with a shield-shaped lock escutcheon (formerly silver plated). This tea caddy would have been perfect for travelling, as it was light in weight, secure and handsome in its form and material. (970.724.1 (A&B))   **by E. Brett Sherlock**

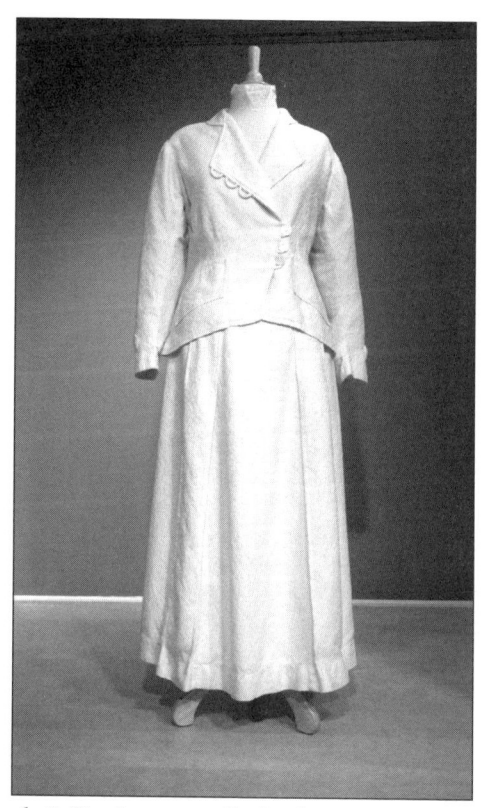

Jacquard "Tailor-made" Costume or Suit circa 1907 – Ball Collection
La Belle Époque 1895-1914, Edwardian Fashion

This is an interesting example of a stylish and sophisticated suit that would be worn to summer weddings or receptions, such as the opening of Memorial Hall in Niagara-on-the-Lake, June 4, 1907.

The skirt is the new (1907) skirt style, full but smooth over the hips and is gored with self panel inserts. The result was a straightened silhouette, which also allowed shoes to show beneath.

The jacket, which is open at the neck, was likely worn with a lovely embellished blouse, as high necks were usual during the day. At night, stylish women wore very décolleté evening dresses with huge leg of mutton sleeves, and jewellery. The jacket is short and softly tailored with a shorter diagonal closing and matching front diagonal pockets. Beautiful details include button closures, pearl buttons and a half belt holding fabric folds at the back above the waist. The overall result was elegant and fashionable.

The costume was worn with a large brimmed hat, often trimmed with feathers extending beyond the brim. Hats were very elaborate and were called Merry Widow hats after the operetta so popular then.

Although handbags were not often carried because money was not needed and cosmetics were rarely worn, parasols were usually carried in the daytime. Shown here is a silk one with little trim – many parasols had more ornamentation such as lace.

Gloves were worn all seasons. The pair likely worn with our suit were lace trim, net fabric instead of the usual washable white kid or elaborately embroidered others. (972.117.1 (A&B))

by Donna Scott, O.C.

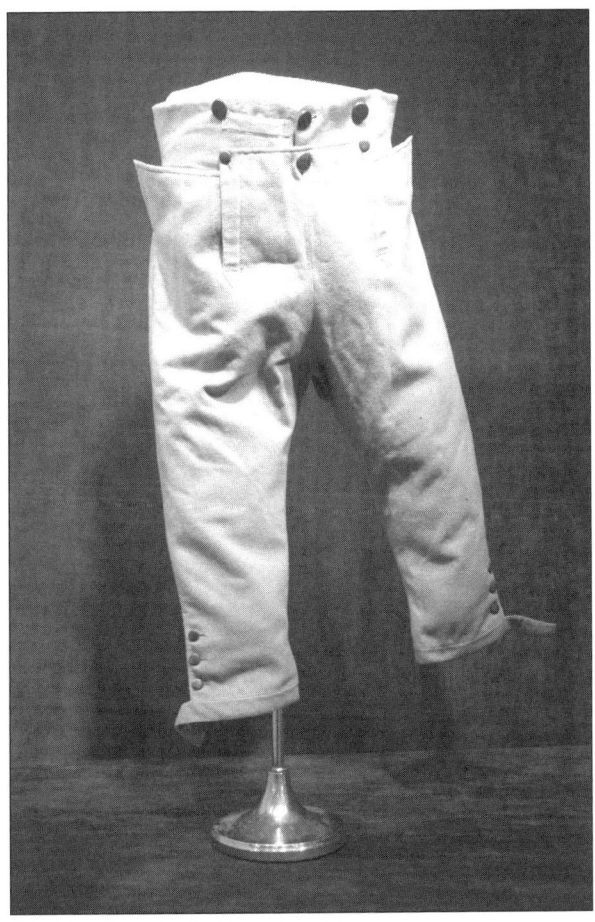

George Bell's Breeches

Alfred Ball's numerous donations of family relics of "early times" to the Niagara Historical Society Museum include these wool breeches. Their original owner, George Ball, was born in Schoharie, N.Y. in 1765, and moved to Upper Canada as a United Empire Loyalist. He served in the War of 1812, was a partner in the establishment of Ball's Mills, and was the original recipient of General Sir Isaac Brock's cocked hat. In his declining years George lived at Locust Grove in Niagara-on-the-Lake.

The melton breeches are tan in colour with a brown triangular shaped piece on the back of the waistband. Though the colour is faded, more protected areas reveal the original rich hue. Wear marks on the breeches are absent. Inserts in the lower back and crotch and tapered legs with buttons and a tab indicate tailoring for a snug fit. The 1810s style breeches were more fitted and length extended to the knee where stockings or high boots covered the lower leg. Metal buttons fastened the drop front and would have held suspenders. Large pockets on either side appear to have a wing detail because of a two inch extension of the pocket above its outside seam. One small pocket on the front right side presumably housed a watch. Buttons are reinforced and the inner waist band measuring 34 inches is lined with linen. The shorter jacket front of this period dictated a higher waistline and drop front to cover the fly. Approaching 1820, fashion changed in favour of full length trousers. (972.179.1)   **by Sara Buyers-Olgivie**

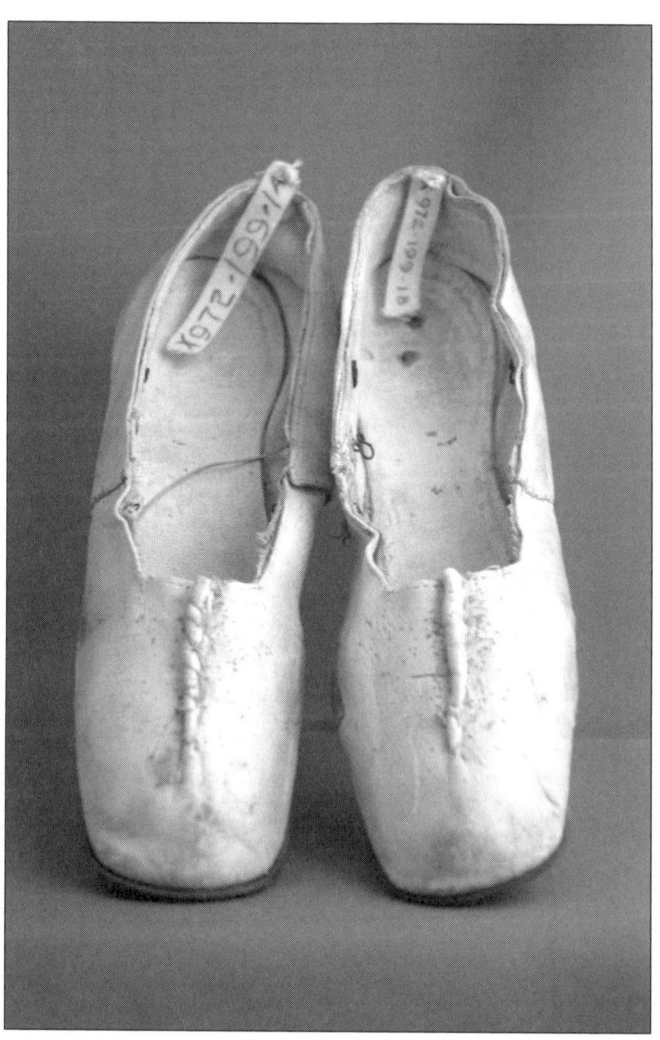

Shoes

These early nineteenth century, kid-leather shoes with their hand-stitched repair, reflect the dramatic change in footwear styles following the French revolution. The high-heeled shoes associated with the aristocracy were abandoned following the conflict, in favour of flat leather slippers. The plain, low-walled shoes contrast sharply with the heavily-embellished silk footwear worn by the upper classes prior to 1790; in fact, the simple style reflected the post-revolution ideal of equality, and it soon spread from Paris to the New World. The long-wearing slippers, which could be easily mended, remained in style, with variations in toe shape, until the advent of the hoop skirt at mid-century.

The Niagara Historical Museum is home to a bounty of interesting footwear – from rare wooden pattens to nineteenth century Adelaides, Garibadis, wedding slippers decorated with Fenelon bows or mother-of-pearl buckles, and richly embellished silk ball slippers. But these ivory, kid-leather flats with their unpretentious patch, are intriguing. Who made them? Who wore them? Where were they purchased? What historical events did they take part in? Why were they repaired and not replaced? For what reason were they preserve, and ultimately donated to the museum? (972.199.1 (A&B)) **by Norma Shephard**

Patten

How many times have you heard the phrase "she is a slipshod housekeeper" or "that work is slipshod?" I was intrigued to discover the derivation offered in Lorraine O'Byrne's (former curator of Black Creek Pioneer Village) booklet, *What is it?* The picture showed a farm woman "slippershod," elevated some five centimetres on top of pattens: two oval iron rings separated by two struts under a thin wooden sole with leather straps tied over the instep. Her skirt and petticoats were lifted and the slippers saved from dirt or snow when she gardened or collected eggs from coop or root cellar. Upper class women with servants went out for walks outdoors. Neither beaded moccasins nor silk slippers stand up to the ground without pattens.

Pattens are centuries old. Elizabeth Semmelhack (curator, Bata Shoe Museum) explained that the dating depends on the sole's toe shape: almond shaped in the 1760s to pointier towards 1800 and squarish from 1800–1850s. Ours are most likely from the 1770s or 1780s. Wooden shoes and clogs were universal. Colonial "wedding shoes" – leather sole, instep, and wooden 5-7cm heel covered with brocade – needed clogs to lift all off the dirt so the shoes could last for church and parties.

As the horses needed "shoes" to prevent slipping, so the shoemakers needed blacksmiths to create pattens. They were practical and saved our pioneer women from being merely slippershod (slipshod) to having better footwear for all the hard work needed. (972.258)

by Elizabeth Oliver-Malone

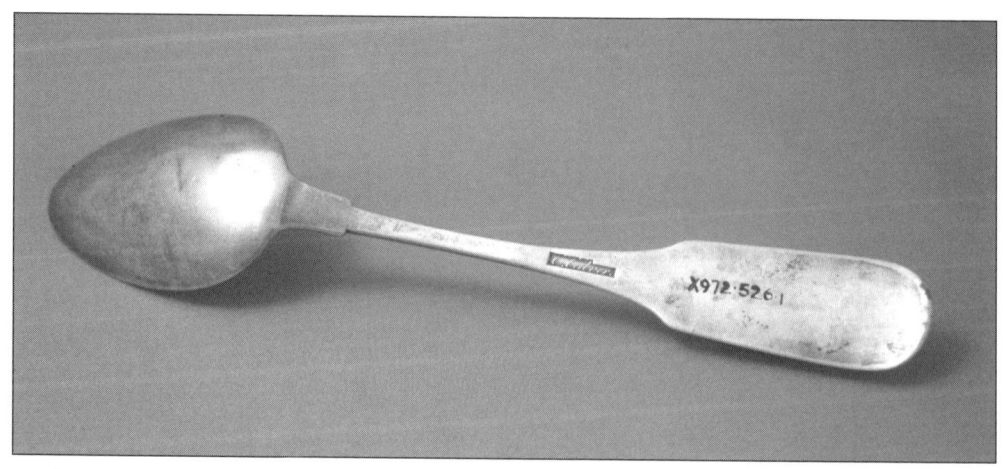

Culver & Wagstaffe Spoons

Elizabeth Showers Ball died December 15, 1855, aged 81. "She was one of the first residents of Upper Canada, and was probably the last survivor of those who were in Fort Wyoming (Pennsylvania) for protection when relieved by the British Army." Elizabeth, daughter of Loyalist Michael and Hannah Showers, was the second wife of Peter Mann Ball (1755 – 1836), who, according to family history, "was the first of the family to enter Canada bringing 60 men from Pennsylvania [Fort Wyoming] at his own expense in 1776." Elizabeth's father and husband were members of Butler's Rangers. One of the founding families of Upper Canada, Ball family members were extensive landowners throughout the Niagara region.

In her Last Will and Testament, Elizabeth left "six large silver tablespoons" to her son William Michael Ball, and "three silver desert spoons, two silver salt spoons" to her son John Clement Ball. Three of the tablespoons engraved "PB" and one small spoon engraved "EB" were donated to the Niagara Historical Society and Museum by descendants of Peter and Elizabeth.

The hallmark, a script "C. Culver", is that of Chester Culver, an early silversmith and merchant in Niagara. Canadian silver expert John Langdon says Culver was in business with John Wagstaff (Wagstaff & Culver, 1817 – 1819), but not by himself, which points to the potential that these spoons are rare.

Culver, who lived with Susannah "three quarters of a mile from the town of Niagara, on the River Road," died in1856, "highly esteemed in all relations in life as an intelligent, admirable and honorable man." (972.526.1)

by Jim Bratton

Board of Ordnance Uniform

This handsome navy blue uniform was a donation from the Hamilton family, descendants of Alexander Hamilton, Sheriff of Upper Canada and builder/owner of the famous Willowbank mansion in Queenston. Records identify it as a dress uniform of junior officer's rank for the Royal Artillery of the period 1840 to 1850, and as having belonged to a Mr. Duff. At first it seemed certain that it belonged to Alexander Duff who married Jessie Augusta, daughter of the late Alexander Hamilton, at Queenston in early 1843. This looked very promising and a search began for information about Alexander.

Mr. Ron Dale, Superintendent, Niagara Historic Sites of Canada, undertook to inspect the uniform to ensure that its identification was correct. He noted that the inscription on the brass buttons was not consistent with the Artillery, but was more likely Board of Ordnance. From this information came the discovery of William Duff, Barracks Master at Fort Malden (Amerherstburg) in the period 1833 to 1837 and brother of the Alexander Duff who married Jessie Hamilton. We are confident that the uniform, now thought to be the finest surviving example of its kind, is that of William Duff and not of Alexander.

(977.8) **by Jim Armstrong**

Cooper Photograph

James Cooper was born in Scotland in 1770. In 1774, his mother Janet, the widow of James Cooper Sr., and her two young sons, Thomas (1767) and James, set sail for America. Janet's brothers, Thomas and John McMicking, were established near Albany, New York. On June 5, 1779, Natives raided their farm and took the family prisoners. The men were taken to Fort Niagara, where ransom was paid for their release. It was several more years before they were able to pay for the release of Janet Cooper and her two sons.
Janet later married William Brown, and she and her two sons moved to Niagara Falls. James married Elizabeth Hixon, who immigrated to Canada in 1788. They raised a large family on their property, which was mid-way between Queenston and Newark. James served as a lieutenant in the War of 1812, where he led the Coloured Corps.
St. Andrew's Presbyterian Church was burned by the Americans in 1813. When the congregation was ready to rebuild, James Cooper's plan was chosen, and the building was completed in 1831. St. Andrew's is described as "an architectural gem".
Janet Carnochan wrote at the time of his death, "Mr. Cooper was one of the sterling men of old times, full of truthfulness, honesty and loyalty." (984.1.169) **by Joan Cooper Elliott**

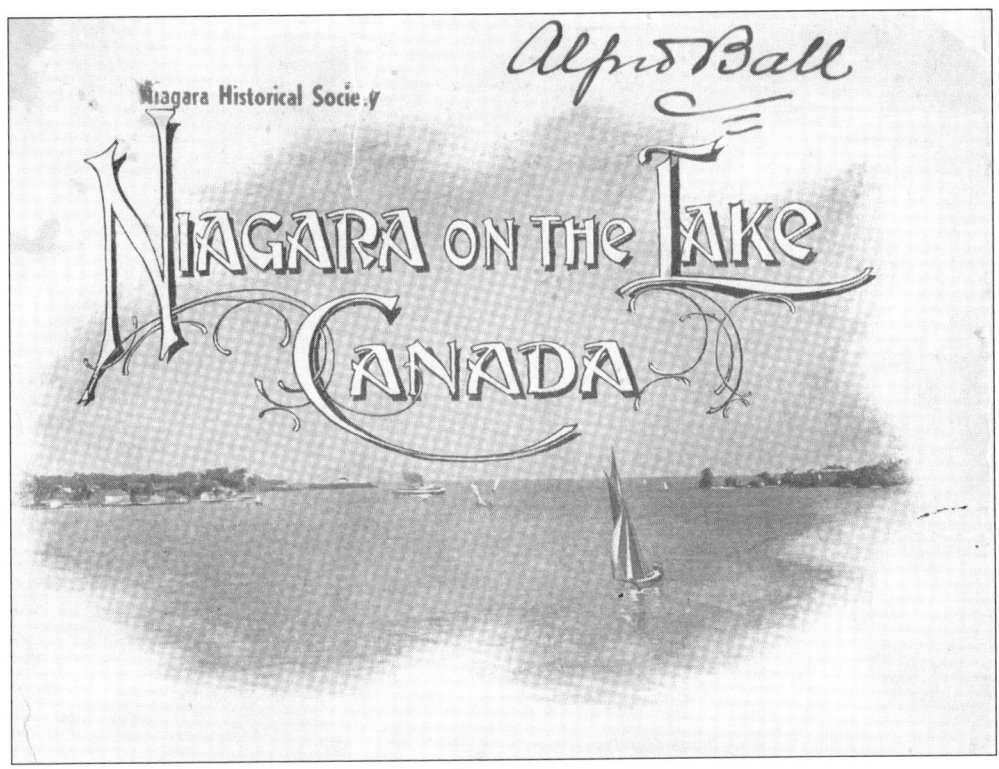

Niagara on the Lake Tourism Brochure
In Search of a Holiday

The cynical voices of the twenty-first century look down upon any advertising that uses more than a handful words to communicate its message. However, when we reach back to 1897 we find the charm of a travel brochure for the Town of Niagara-on-the-Lake.

"After perusal of this booklet – rest assured you will find that neither your time or your money has been misspent ... The one spot on this American Continent where nature has joined hands with man for the common purpose of making all things beautiful ... within an hour's ride by train, steamer or electric car from Buffalo or Niagara Falls."

Now that it has your interest, what is there to do? "Fishing for bass, pickerel, perch and herring ... Quiet anchorage for your yacht, no matter what the weather the boating is safe ... horseback riding or for those devotees of the wheel, safe smooth hard gravel roads ... Visit the historic battlefields in the neighbourhood, recalling the days of Simcoe and Brock, and at the Queen's Royal, the popular Saturday evening 'Hops'."

Then comes the promotion of sports of the day: "tennis, lawn bowling and golf, where Niagara-on-the-Lake is headquarters for these fascinating sports, make the hours slip by on golden wings of pleasure."

Now for those who wanted some peace and quiet we read: "The zephyrs sing softly in the trees o'er head and the sweet scented air, the gently swaying branches, and lovetwitters of the birds, seem to combine in the labour of lulling you into a calm and delicious languor."

All of this charm comes at a price, and in further reading we learn: "leave no stone unturned, and spare no expense, to provide guests with the best of everything. The rates at this hotel are from $2.50 a day up." Holiday anyone? (985.4.488) **by Janet James**

Fire Insurance Plaque

In Upper Canada during the early nineteenth century fire insurance companies provided metal plaques to homeowners who had purchased insurance coverage. The sample plaque in the Museum's collection is an oval 18x14 cm. It depicts two hands shaking at the top centre above the date 1836, followed by the words "Niagara District Mutual Fire Insurance Co." The plaque is made of iron and is faded green, yellow, brown and black in colour.

Open fires were an essential part of living in those days, used for heating in winter and cooking throughout the year. But with many fires often unprotected and unguarded, and many houses made almost entirely of wood, serious fires were quite common and often devastating. The homeowner displayed the plaque on the outside of his house so that fire fighters, arriving to extinguish the fire, would see the plaque and know that they would be paid by the insurance company upon successful completion of their job. It is said that fire brigades would sometimes refuse to put out a fire if there was no immediate evidence of fire insurance on the property.

Indeed, fire was so ever-present and potentially catastrophic at that time that it became common for many insurance companies to own and operate their own fire brigades until that responsibility was passed over to local government in 1866.

In Niagara-on-the-Lake there is one known fire insurance plaque on a house dating from those times. It is at The Whale Inn, adjacent to the Niagara River at the junction of King and Delater streets. The plaque (in an "upright" oval shape) is visible from the road, located above the door at the rear of the building. (986.1.523) **by Elizabeth Surtees**

Box of Eliza Morris

The words "orphan," "workhouse," and "child migration" conjure up heart-wrenching images of hardship, loneliness and premature loss of the treasured protective veil of childhood. All of these words are contained in the historical documents related to the operations of Miss Maria Rye, who oversaw the emigration of destitute children from the UK to Canada during the period 1869 to 1895. During those years, Miss Rye, an ardent supporter of women's rights and employment, was responsible for the emigration of over 1100 children – children who were taken from their unfortunate, rough beginnings to the farmlands surrounding Niagara, where they started new lives.

In Niagara, the children were received at "Our Western Home," the original Court House and Jail on Rye Street, where Miss Rye maintained a home for the new arrivals. Applications were received from local families who were interested in hiring these children and many of them were brought up as "one of the family," helping to farm and develop Niagara's agricultural areas.

The privilege of actually being able to see one of the children's shipping trunks at the Museum, with the inscription, "Eliza Morris. Care of Miss Rye, Niagara, Canada" carefully written on its side, indeed makes one feel grateful for all that we have.

Every time I look at the trunk, I wonder … did Eliza write her own name on the trunk – with great anticipation of the unknown that lay ahead of her? Or, if someone else wrote her name with such great care, why did their care not extend to keeping Eliza with them? Or were they making a tough choice – a choice to send Eliza to what would likely be a better life in Canada? So much can be read into the inscription that is written in such beautiful, careful penmanship.

What a wonderful piece of Niagara's history – so simple, yet capable of eliciting so many questions, so much emotion. (986.1.54) **by Janice Thomson**

Photograph of the Royal Party 1901

The royal tour of the Duke and Duchess of Cornwall and York, 16 March 1901 to 1 November 1901, was undertaken for several reasons: to assert the pivotal role of the monarch as the unifying force of the Empire; to thank those countries which had contributed forces to the war in South Africa, which was still being fought; and to open the first parliament of the new Commonwealth of Australia. The tour had been postponed by the death of Queen Victoria in January, 1901 but was actively promoted by the Secretary for the Colonies, Mr Joseph Chamberlain, and the First Lord of the Treasury, Mr Arthur Balfour, despite the misgivings of the new king, Edward VII.

The Duke and Duchess visited Australia, South Africa, and Canada, landed at Quebec on 16 September, and remained in Canada for a month. Accompanied by the Governor General, the 4th Earl of Minto, and Prime Minister Sir Wilfred Laurier for part of their journey, the royal couple visited Montreal, Ottawa, Winnipeg, Regina, Calgary, Vancouver, Victoria, Toronto, Niagara, St John, Halifax, and St John's. Accompanying them as well were twelve officials of the Royal Household for the Duke and seven officials for the Duchess. Among them were the Duchess's brother, Prince Alexander of Teck, as an aide-de-camp who later became the Earl of Athlone and Governor General of Canada, 1939-1945. One of the Duke's equerries was the Hon. Derek Keppel, whose mother was the daughter of Sir Alan MacNab of Hamilton, Ontario. She had married her husband, later the 7th Earl of Albemarle, at Dundurn Castle in Hamilton. (Mr Derek Keppel's sister-in-law, the Hon. Mrs George Keppel, was Edward VII's mistress, and the great-grandmother of the present Duchess of Cornwall.)

The tour was a huge success for the monarchy and Empire and for the maturing of the Duke of Cornwall into his royal role. On November 9, 1901, the Duke's father, King Edward VII, named him Prince of Wales. As George V (1910-1936) he succeeded his father as king nine years later. (986.14B) **by James Mainprize**

18th Century Girl's Corset

A piece such as this corset is important to the Museum's collection and is particularly interesting because clothing was a valuable commodity in eighteenth century Niagara. Cloth was imported and quite costly and professional corset makers were often employed because of a corset's precise construction. The corset also tells a story about the values and practices of eighteenth century society.

This corset (or stay), circa 1780, is made of linen with wooden stays and laces at the back. Other examples used whalebone to create structure. The main purpose of the corset was to create a small waist and a raised bust. It was common belief that women were to "train" the body from a young age in order to obtain the desired hour-glass figure of the period. However, this look did not come without consequence. Many women experienced painful effects of long-term wear including problems with breathing, deformed bone structure and shifting of the organs. It is seen as a torturous and inhumane practice of the past, but the ideals of the corset have not completely disappeared in our society. Many women use devices to create a smaller waist (using lycra and spandex) and some even use surgical means to obtain a slimmer look.

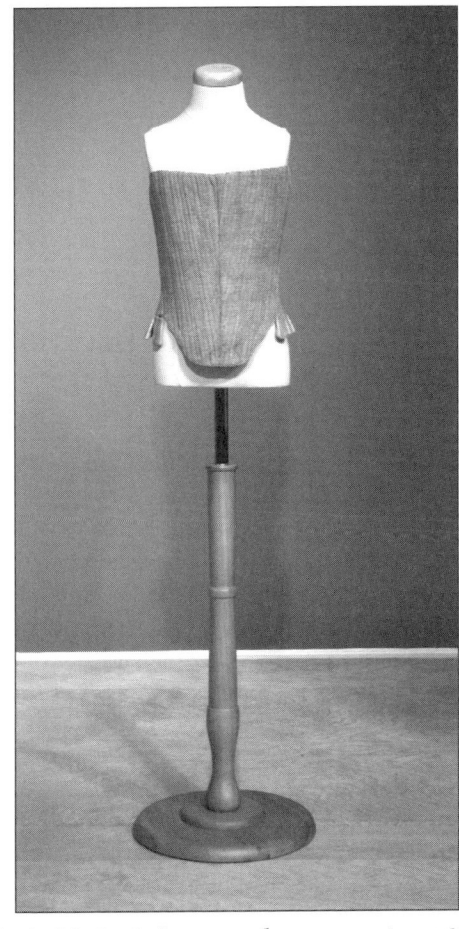

Since corsets were ultimately used to create a desirable look for men, they were viewed as a symbol of women's inferior status. As the corset has come and gone throughout twentieth century fashion in various forms, many now see it not as a symbol of oppression, but have reclaimed it as an artistic symbol of female beauty and empowerment. (986.3.1)

by Amy Klassen

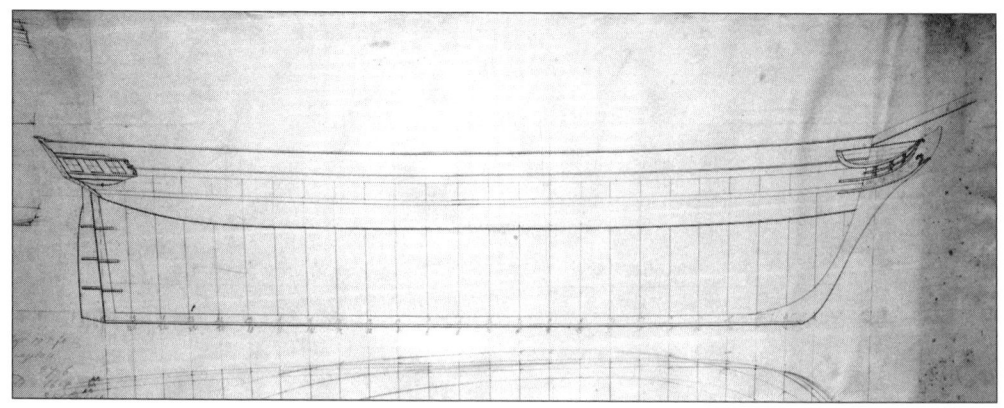

Gilkison Ship Plans

Robert Gilkison was born in Queenston in 1810, the fourth son of William Gilkison and Isabella Grant. William had been Master of a schooner on Lake Erie for the Aster Fur Interests. He "swallowed the anchor" in 1803 and settled in Queenston to manage his father-in-law's forwarding business. His mother also had a marine background as her father, Alexander Grant, had commanded the British fleet on the lakes in 1757.

The family returned to Scotland in 1815 so that the boys could be educated. Robert finished school in 1825 and was apprenticed to Mr. John Wood, the leading builder of steamships on the Clyde, including the Comet of 1812. Young Robert must have been pleased to learn from such a talented builder, who was operating at the cutting edge of the industry. He completed his apprenticeship in 1831 and moved to Liverpool.

The drawings in the collection date from the latter part of his apprenticeship and must be considered a student portfolio. They are done with various levels of skill and some are incomplete. My favourite is the "Royal George," a set of lines with a very pleasing form. Another one I like is the "Hearts of Oak" which shows a fanciful figurehead, indicating that he was subject to daydreaming, a common trait of ship designers.

Robert was appointed shipbuilder to the Niagara Dock Company in 1835, but only stayed five years before returning to Scotland, where he died in 1855.   (987.5.007 - 987.5.016)

by R.C. Johnston

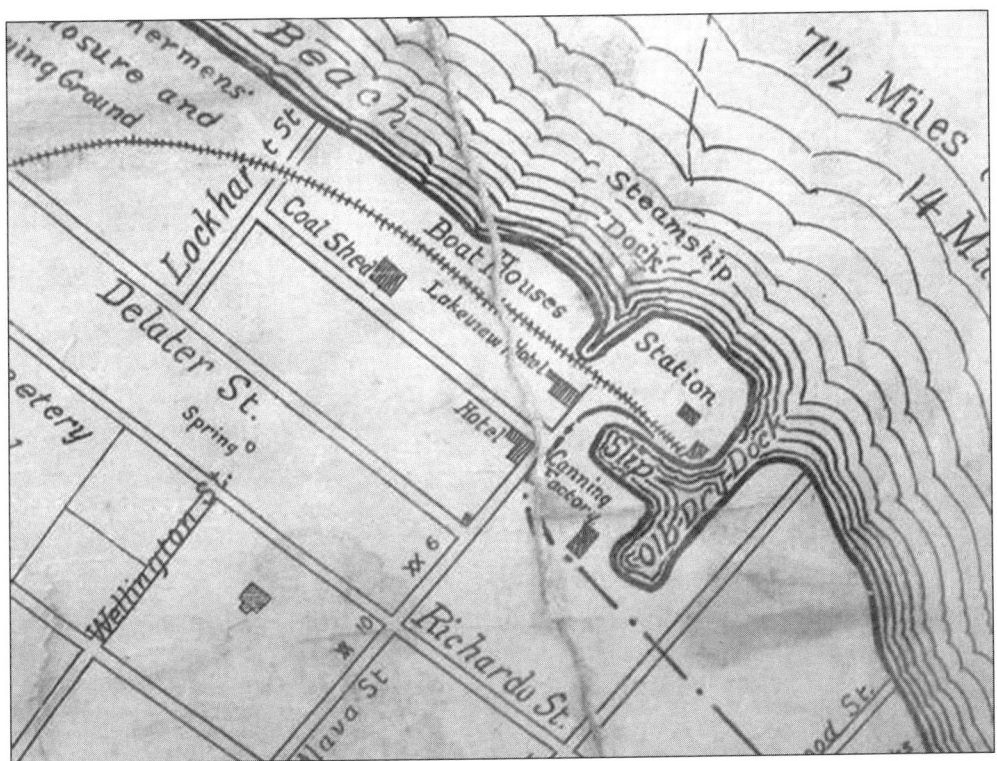

Souvenir Map 1894

The Souvenir Historical Map of the Town of Niagara, County of Lincoln, Ontario was compiled and drawn by Frank Johnson, published in June 1894 and priced at $2.00.

This map gives us the opportunity to compare Then with Now – for example:

1. At the mouth of One Mile Creek

Then: A hotel is shown on a body of water grandly named "Lake Como."

Now: The hotel site is a private residence overlooking a languid pond bisected by Niagara Blvd.

2. Between the foot of King Street and the foot of Lockhart Street

Then: A Sandy Beach.

Now: Lockhart Street does not even exist and, as a result of the approximate 4-foot rise in Lake Ontario as a consequence of the building of the St. Lawrence Seaway in the 1950s, the sandy beach no longer exists either.

3. At the foot of Gate Street in the grounds of the lakeside Queen's Royal Hotel

Then: A "Believers Pavilion" whose purpose and role is shrouded in mystery.

Now: The site is adjacent to the Niagara Golf Club's clubhouse, which is frequented, ironically, by those who are also "believers" – in their own ability as golfers.

4. Close to the junction of King Street and Delater Street

Then: A natural spring used, it is said, by townsfolk for fresh water year 'round.

Now: The spring is still there and quite visible from the street, but used only for garden watering by the homeowner upon whose property it is located. (987.5.018)   **by David Murray**

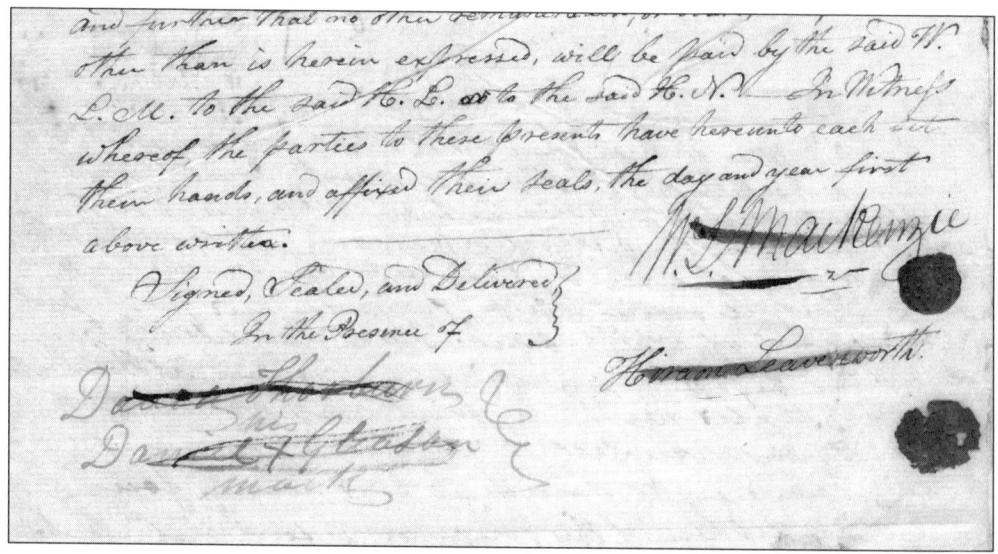

Mackenzie–Leavenworth Indenture Agreement

William Lyon Mackenzie had been editing his *Colonial Advocate* newspaper in Queenston for three months when, in 1824, he took a step crucial to his and Upper Canada's political future. Instead of weekly contracting out his printing to Oliver Grace across the river in Lewiston, Mackenzie lured from Rochester Hiram Leavenworth – along with his "Press, types and printing materials" – to Queenston "to conduct, manage and carry on" a printing business on Mackenzie's behalf. This is Mackenzie's original copy of the six-month agreement that details Leavenworth's duties and salary, and the possible purchase by Mackenzie of all the equipment. It was "signed, sealed, and delivered," witnessed by David Thorburn and Daniel Gleason ("his mark") on August 23, 1824; Leavenworth the next day bonded himself for "one hundred and five pounds lawful money." Within a month, the printshop was in full operation in Mackenzie's Queenston home, thus confirming that the *Colonial Advocate* was no passing fancy but was destined to become an enduring influence. (987.5.082)

by Chris Raible

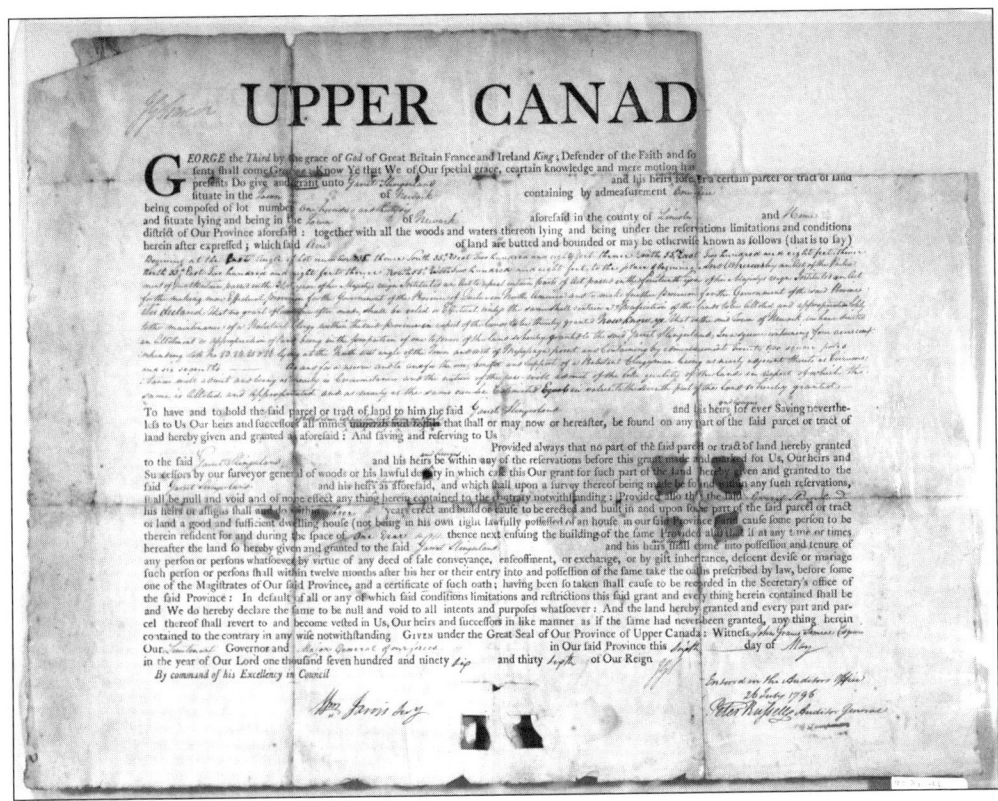

Garret Slingerland Land Grant – July 26, 1796

On July 26, 1796 Garret Slingerland was granted a one-acre lot, #136 located on the northwest corner of Gage and Butler Streets in the town of Newark, the capital of Upper Canada. This document granted land on behalf of King George III and witnessed by John Graves Simcoe.

Garret was a private with his nephew and three brothers in Butler's Rangers. His father was an officer for the Albany Battalion and a war prisoner for quite some time. They originated from Dutch Reform families in Slingerlands N.Y., settling 10,000 acres of land next to Albany N.Y. in 1654. Garret's family could not remain or return to the U.S. and thus became part of the loyalist migration to Canada.

The Land Grant is one of many received by Garret in recognition of his military service and for loss of lands and property in the American Revolution. These grants required support for the clergy to one seventh of the value of the land, and a requirement to build a house and occupy it within three years. Garret was one of the original 324 families that settled Niagara from November 25, 1784 to June 1785. This was a well-conceived plan to move and populate the provinces of Canada with experienced soldier/settlers, able to clear lands and defend them in anticipation of an American invasion that came in 1812. To this day, many members of the Slingerland family still serve the Niagara-on-the-Lake community and farm its lands. (987.5.106)

by Jamie Slingerland

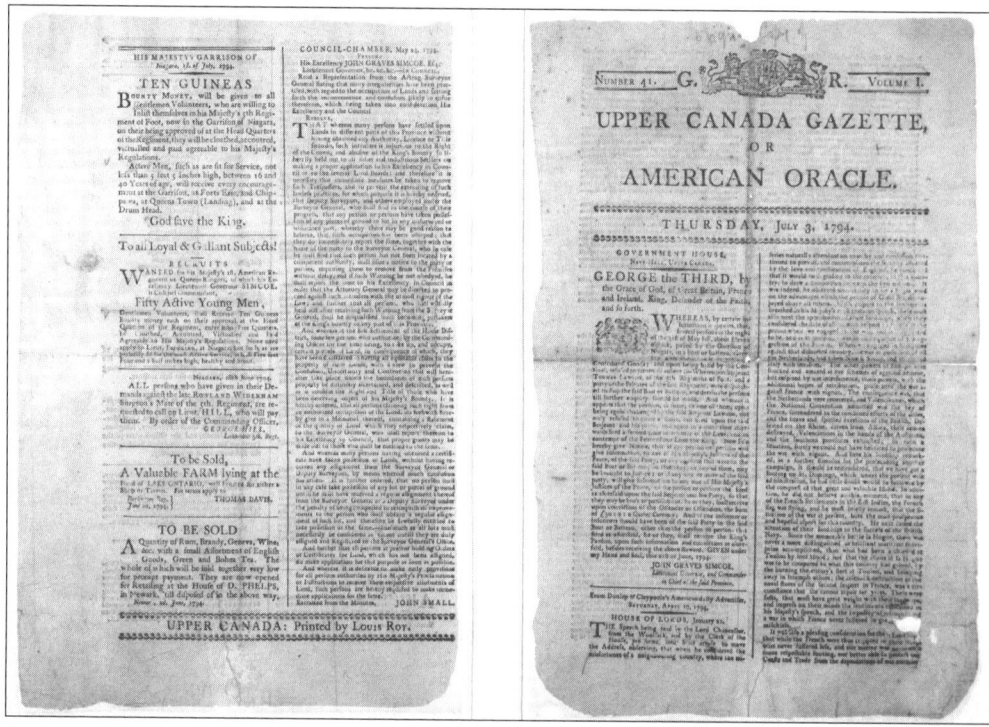

Upper Canada Gazette

The 1911 catalogue of Memorial Hall artefacts describes three issues of the *Upper Canada Gazette*, donated by Charles A.F. Ball from a Loyalist family. In 1792, John Graves Simcoe established the Office of the Printer, whose purpose was to inform the public of government activities. Louis Roy came that fall from Quebec with a second-hand wooden printing press and reams of linen paper. On April 18, 1793, the first *Upper Canada Gazette* appeared. The Museum's issue of July 3, 1794 followed the layout of the *London Gazette* and Simcoe's orders. A mix of official notices and local notices included three enlistment notices, news of smugglers on the river and an ad for a Burlington farm.

The next edition of August 14, 1794 published a proclamation for the opening of Parliament. The complete address by the Bishop of Quebec fills a page along with some news of European events reprinted from Philadelphia papers with little regard for copyright. Louis Roy resigned to return to Montreal and Gideon Tiffany, a journalist from New York, edited the third issue of December 10, 1794. It contains more international news: the guillotining of Robespierre, raising a liberty pole in Baltimore, and the attack on Fort Miami. Tiffany proved too independent and he was dismissed in 1797.

Loyalty to the government was the only qualification for editors. A surgeon, a banker, and a merchant were among those hired. Still, conflicts occurred and in the 50 years of publishing, only four editors left of their own accord. Today, the voice of government, the *Ontario Gazette*, is published online, a far cry from the wooden presses of Simcoe's day.

(987.5.399)

by Nancy Butler

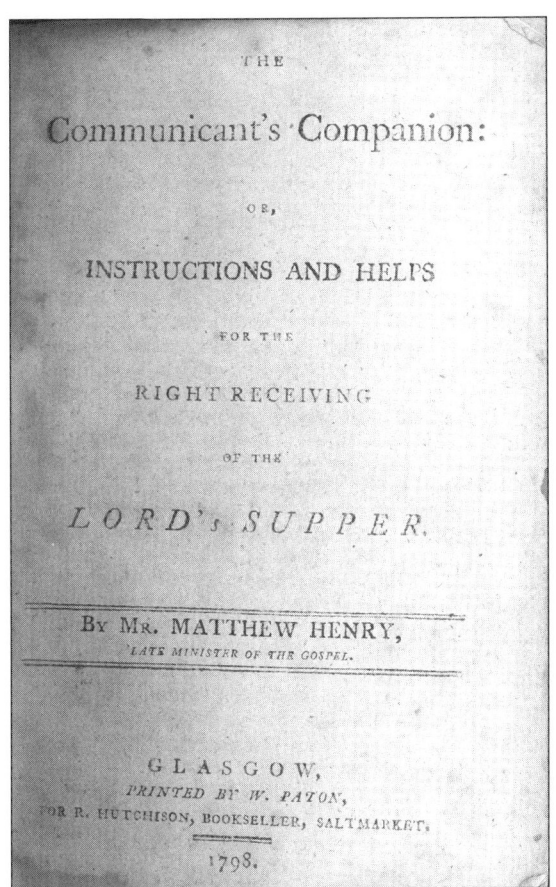

***The Communicants Companion, or Instructions and Helps for the Right Receiving of the Lord's Supper,* by Mr. Matthew Henry, Late Minister of the Gospel**

Published in Glasgow in 1798, this is one of only two known books from the collection of the original Niagara Library, still located in our community. It is listed as No. 81 in the handwritten catalogue of the early library's holdings. The bookplate reads "Niagara Library 1801" and its purchase price was 4 shillings.

The library was founded on June 8, 1800 when forty-one prominent Niagara residents met to form a subscription library, which they named the Niagara Library. "Sensible how much we are at a loss in this new and remote country for every kind of useful knowledge," the subscribers resolved, "and convinced that nothing would be of more use to diffuse knowledge amongst us and our offspring, than a library, supported by subscription in this town, we, whose names are hereunto subscribed hereby associate ourselves together for that purpose." Andrew Heron (c.1765-1848), a merchant and land speculator resident in Niagara since 1785, was instrumental in the library's organization.

The library flourished and by late 1812 offered 827 volumes to its subscribers. However, after the American forces withdrew and burned the town on December 13, 1813 only about 200 books remained and the original Niagara Library was forced to cease operations in 1820. We are so fortunate to still have this book at the Museum as a reminder of our history and of the value placed by our forefathers on establishing a library in our community. (987.5.4.17)

by Gerda Molson

> **PROCLAMATION.**
> Province of Upper Canada.
>
> ISAAC BROCK, Esquire, President adminiſtering the Government of the Province of Upper Canada, and Major-General Commanding His Majesty's Forces within the same.
>
> TO ALL TO WHOM IT MAY CONCERN :—.GREETING.
>
> WHEREAS information has been received, that divers perſons have recently come into this Province, with a seditious intent to diſturb the tranquility thereof, and to endeavour to alienate the minds of His Majeſty's Subjects from His Perſon and Government ; I hereby require and enjoin the several perſons authorized, to carry into effect a certain Statute, paſſed in the Forty-fourth year of his Majeſty's reign, intituled, "An Act for the better securing this Province againſt all seditious attempts or designs to diſturb the tranquility thereof," to be vigilant in the execution of their duty, and ſtrictly to enquire into the behaviour and conduct of all ſuch persons as may be subject to the provisions of the said Act; and I do also charge and require all his Majeſty's Good and Loyal Subjects within this Province, to be aiding and assiſting the said Perſons, in the execution of the powers veſted in them by the said Act.
>
> GIVEN under my Hand and Seal at Arms, at York, this Twenty-fourth day of February, in the year of our Lord One thousand Eight hundred and Twelve, and in the Fifty-second of his Majeſty's Reign.
>
> ISAAC BROCK, Preſident.
>
> *By Command of His Honor,*
> WM. JARVIS, Sec'y.

Brock Proclamation

I was intrigued by the proclamation sent out by Major General Isaac Brock to the residents of Upper Canada. The context for the proclamation was the news that war had broken out between the United States and Great Britain. As one of Britain's colonies, this meant that we were at war with the United States.

I believe the proclamation served two purposes. It quickly established that the British authority would continue to have civil and military jurisdiction within the colony and that the territory needed to be on a heightened state of alert for individuals that might threaten the well-being of Upper Canada. More importantly though, it sent the message that Britain was here to stay and was determined to maintain Upper Canada as part of the British Empire.

The War of 1812 occurred only three decades after the conclusion of the American Revolutionary War. Many individuals on both sides of the border believed it was inevitable that Canada would eventually become part of the American Republic. The actions of General Brock reassured the citizens that Britain was absolutely committed to their well-being and the continuation of Upper Canada under the British flag.

Brock's proclamation had the desired effect, as there are examples at every major confrontation, of local citizens and aboriginal communities actively supporting the British cause.

The War of 1812 settled once and for all the fact that North America would be divided between American and British interests. There was no serious challenge to that *status quo* after the war, due in part to General Brock's quick action to establish control within the colony. (987.5.463)

by Hon. Rob Nicholson, MP

Theatre Programme

This is the playbill from a performance of a melodrama, "Kathleen Mavourneen" at the Music Hall in Niagara-on-the-Lake in March of 1915. The cast features such classic character types as Father O'Cassidy, Black Rody and Red Barney. The action appears to involve a dastardly plan to kidnap young Kathleen, who is apparently rescued from this perhaps-worse-than-death fate by the worthy Terrence O'More.

The ads in the program offer an intriguing snapshot of 1915 Niagara-on-the-Lake – hotel rooms "lighted by electricity" for $1.50; good cheap liquor at the Niagara Liquor Store; French Bons Bons from Henry Evans and Lemon Bars at 3 dozen for 25 cents. This program also features a notice from the commander, T.F Best, that Labrador Herring and Quail on Toast are to be "sacrificed" during the Lenten season in order to increase supplies for the Front.

Colleen and I found this playbill of great interest, not only for its theatrical history, but also for the fact that my grandfather, Lieutenant James Forgie, who was at that time in training here in Niagara-on-the-Lake with the 92nd Battalion of the 48th Highlanders, may well have taken in this performance. It is also possible that he was accompanied by my grandmother, whom he had recently met. They had been introduced the previous summer, when she and many other debutantes came over on the steamship from Toronto to socialize with the soldiers. They were secretly married before he left for the front and she followed him to France, where he served on the Somme and she drove an ambulance. They later had a formal second wedding for the benefit of the parents.

(987.5.472) **by Christopher & Colleen Blake**

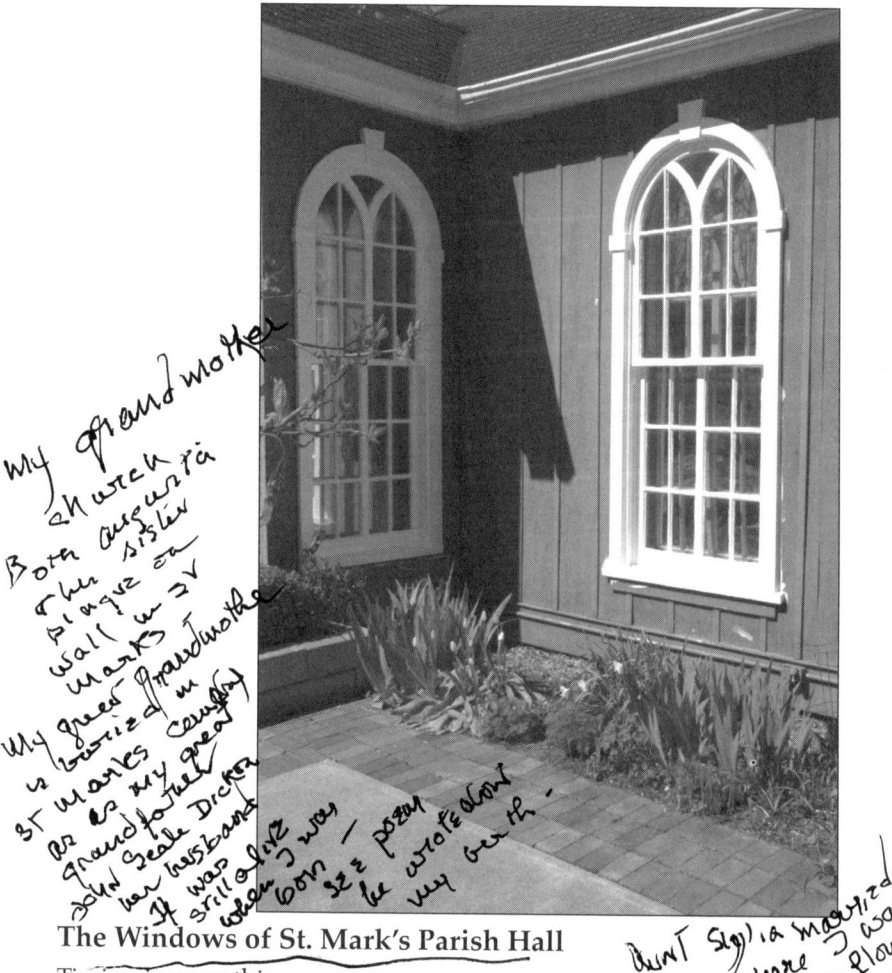

The Windows of St. Mark's Parish Hall

Timing is everything.

St. Mark's Parish Hall was completed in 1887. By 1966 the facility was inadequate to serve the expanding congregation. So the noted restoration architect, Peter Stokes, designed wings to be built along both sides of the existing building. What had been the side windows became doorways and thus eight very large windows were left sitting useless in a builder's yard.

Memorial Hall, built in 1907, was the original museum. When it was decided to link this to the adjacent vacant high school building constructed in 1875, Paul Johns prepared the plans. Remembering that St. Mark's had eight surplus windows and that the Museum needed windows, he had an idea. It was a solution made in heaven. It must have given everyone deep satisfaction knowing that two problems had been solved. How elegant the windows looked in their new location. The design provided a perfect marriage between the gothic High School building and the Neo Classic feel of the Museum building.

This is so characteristic of Niagara-on-the-Lake. St. Mark's chandeliers grace Drope Hall in the Court House and the pinnacles from St. Mark's tower for many years supported a garden swing until they rotted away.

Among the artefacts in the collection of the Museum, the provenance of these elegant, old windows is my favourite.

by Donald Combe

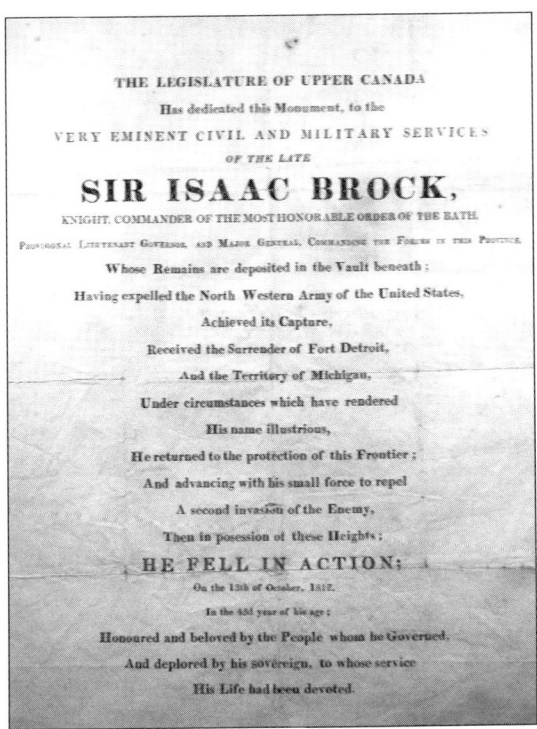

Handbill

A handbill hangs behind glass at the Niagara Historical Museum, printed by William Lyon Mackenzie and announcing the burial of Sir Isaac Brock. But which burial? In addition to Brock's numerous accomplishments as much-revered general of the Battle of Queenston Heights, he has the distinction of being buried four times.

After his death on October 13, 1812 while repelling American invaders, Brock was carried to his first resting place by a military procession to one of the bastions at Fort George. But it was decided the hero of Upper Canada deserved a more suitable memorial, and in 1824, after much discussion about design, construction was begun on a monument, with a vault to house his remains.

Meanwhile, Mackenzie had begun printing his politically controversial newspaper in Queenston, and used his press to announce the second funeral for Brock, "honoured and beloved by the people." The elaborate ceremony attended by thousands was held October 13, 1824, 12 years exactly after Brock's death.

That vault beneath the monument, however, was not to be his final resting place. In 1840, the structure was damaged by a gunpowder bomb planted by someone seeking retribution for a relative killed by the British. The remains of Brock were moved to the Hamilton family cemetery on the grounds of Willowbank in Queenston, until they could be reinterred in 1853, on October 13, the 41st anniversary of the battle, and carried up the hill to another vault beneath the reconstructed monument, during another solemn ceremony again attended by thousands paying their respects to the fallen war hero.

In 2006, the monument temporarily closed for renovations, Highway 405 was renamed the General Brock Parkway, again on October 13, as another tribute and a reminder of Brock's contribution to history for all who pass by the 210-foot memorial towering above the escarpment and over the earthly remains of Sir Isaac Brock. (988.5.158)   **by Penny Coles**

Niagara Dramatic Club Playbill

Simply spending a morning at the Niagara Historical Society and Museum, poring over old posters and playbills (my requested area of exploration) is plunging into a world that is unexpectedly full of energy, creativity and idealism. I say unexpectedly, because I thought that theatre in bygone days in Niagara-on-the-Lake was probably a very formal, polite and "civilized" activity, but I was wrong. The playbill I have chosen is a good example of what I mean.

On Wednesday and Thursday March 25 & 26, 1874, the Niagara Dramatic Club presented a "Great Drama" with the fabulously dramatic title "Self Accusation or, A Brother's Love." I immediately get the sense of a hugely emotional story with a strong dash of adventure, especially noting the inclusion of gamekeepers and constables in the cast list. And then there is the special role played by Prof. C. Kendall, Hercules De Fernessia. How did he fit in?

Not content with one play we also have the "Great Nautical Drama," "Flying Dutchman or the Phantom Ship" with a cast list that includes brilliantly colourful characters such as "Mynheer von Swiggs," "Sinutta" and "Rochalda – an Evil Spirit of the Deep" and this is just a foretaste for the story and synopsis where the description "Vanderdecken walking the deck swearing fearfully" or the extract "Burst stormy clouds and overwhelm them, Rochalda, I come" present wonderfully vital and theatrical images.

As I look at the names of the cast members I see several repeated – not to mention a Mr. F.H. Granger, a local artist apparently, who played several parts and is credited as Manager. A picture of a committed, enthusiastic group evolves. The plays are of a substantial size and certainly in the case of the "Flying Dutchman" must have required some creative production work. Nothing restrained here.

And the audience? Well, for a mere 25 cents (15 for the kids) the denizens of Niagara-on-the-Lake were obviously ready to be swept away into a world of sex, treachery and mystery, something I will keep up my sleeve when next questioned about a potentially racy programming choice. My only question as I reluctantly return to the present day is – who was "Barney the Baron"? (988.5.179)

by Jackie Maxwell

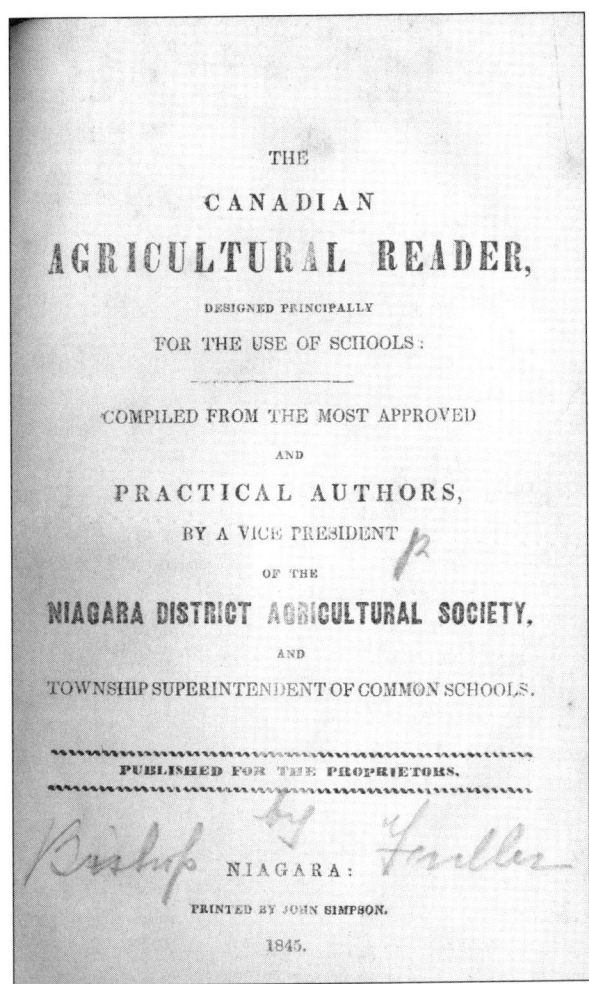

The Canadian Agricultural Reader

This artefact is a rare, early Niagara imprint. Designed as a school text, it combined practical instruction with didactic poetry and fables. Chapters deal with various aspects of husbandry, except fruit growing which was not yet widespread in the region. The contributors were British and American authorities.

The text was edited by Thomas Brock Fuller (1810-1884), Anglican rector of Thorold, archdeacon, and first bishop of Niagara (1875). He was Superintendent of Common Schools, and vice president of the Niagara District and Thorold Agricultural Societies. He married Cynthia, daughter of merchant Samuel Street. Fuller owned The Beechwoods, a house near the site of Beaverdams.

John Simpson (1807-1878) came from Yorkshire to Niagara in 1835. A bookseller and stationer, he published the *Niagara Chronicle* (1837-52), and several books. His business interests included insurance, building societies, plank and railroad companies. He was collector of customs, president of the Board of Police, district and Niagara town councillor, and mayor of Niagara (1852-56). A Conservative member of parliament (1857), he became deputy assistant auditor general (1864). He died in Ottawa, but was interred in St. Mark's Churchyard. (988.5.454)   **by Brian Narhi**

Book of Tickets for Niagara Navigation Company: The Four C's

Pictured is a book of tickets for passage on any one of Canada Steamship Lines's four steamboats for the Niagara division. They were the greatest passenger ships that ever sailed Lake Ontario. Each summer when the steamer S.S. *Cayuga* sailed from Toronto to Niagara on her first trip of the season, children and parents from Niagara were invited for a free trip up the Niagara River to Queenston and back. When the Lions Beach at the foot of King Street was the most popular place for swimming, children looked to the arrival of the *Cayuga* each day so they could play in the large waves she created. The *Cayuga* was Canada Steamship Lines's last and grandest passenger ship in the Niagara fleet. She was 317 feet long and capable of carrying 2,500 passengers and crew. Named after the famous Native tribe, she was in service from 1907 to 1957 and carried 15 million passengers in her lifetime. In 1952, due to a decrease in passengers, Canada Steamships announced they would be taking the *Cayuga* out of service. In the summer of 1953 the *Cayuga* did not run while a group of public stockholders purchased the ship and started the Cayuga Steamship Company. The following year she was back in service. She ran for the next three years, but sadly at the end of the 1957 season she made her final trip. Low ticket sales and increased debt were responsible for the *Cayuga's* decline. In 1961 she was scrapped at Hamilton. (989.052)

by Jim Smith

Reflector Oven

"Why is it that she must be forever superior to us? We can never hope to attain the luxuries that she enjoys"

This plaintive cry echoed from the mildewed, fragile page I had just discovered hidden in the depths of an ancient trunk lurking in the attic of the old building for at least one hundred and fifty years.

Further perusal revealed that the writer was consumed with envy over her sister's purchase of a gleaming new tin kitchen. Apparently, this utensil would prevent flames erupting as a roast dripped into the hearth and, as had tragically happened, ultimately causing several ghastly deaths. According to this letter, such had been the fate of a hapless neighbour's family. A young mother and her children had been unable to escape as the flames had, presumably, leaped into the thatched roof and destroyed their cottage.

This life-saving acquisition could roast meat on its revolving, spring-driven spit and the dangerous drippings could be caught in the drip-pan as it sat, face-forward, close to the glowing hearth. The shining, curved back of this wonder provided the reflective heat for the completion of this possibly hazardous task. With this new "appliance," to use a modern term, life could only be easier and safer for the wealthier, envied sister.

The yellowed page almost seethed with the writer's impotent rage and jealousy as she fulminated about her inability to buy what must have been the contemporary equivalent of a modern microwave oven.

Yet, the comparison of these two domestic objects is not exact. The microwave oven, while easing the job of the cook, does not necessarily save that cook from an unimaginably horrible death, whereas the tin kitchen could well do just that. Our forbears had much to cope with. (989.088)

by Barbara McCarthy

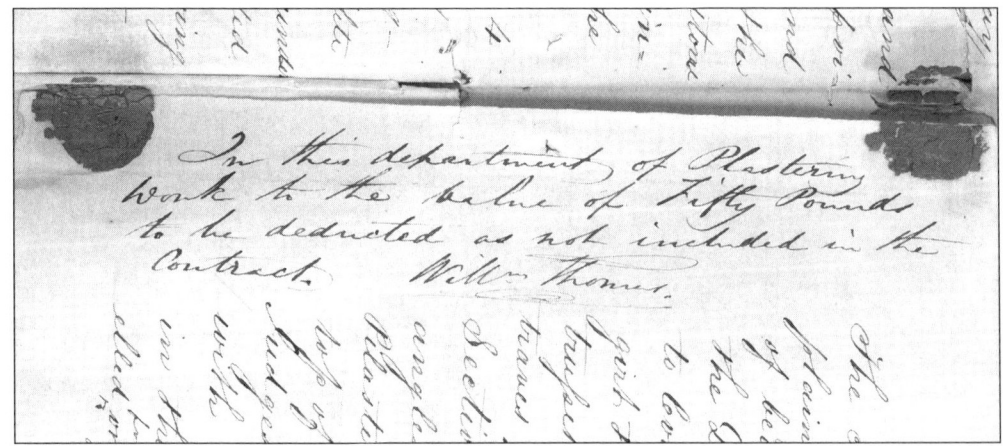

Specifications for the Town Hall, Market House (Court House) – 18, 46, 26 Queen Street

The specifications for the Court House, written by the architect William Thomas and signed on October 8, 1846 by both the architect and contractors who worked on the building, are remarkable for the detailed account they give of the construction techniques and materials that were used and for their insight into the high level of quality workmanship demanded by Thomas. (The detail shows an amendment on the contract price.)

The specifications dealt with excavation, brick and rubble stone work, cut stone work, plaster, carpentry and joinery, plumbing, painting and glazing, and conditions for contractors.

The contractors were required to use "good hard sound burnt brick" and a specific recipe for mortar consisting of "the best fresh burnt lime and good sharp sand mixed one part lime to two parts sand." The architect also required that the stonemasons use "best Queenston or Thorold stone from local quarries" and provided detailed instructions for the construction of the stone walls, arches, portico and window openings.

Today the Court House stands as a testament to the workmanship of men like James Garvie and John Davidson and to the quality of Thomas's design. Completed in just over a year, this Classical Revival building with its carved keystones and elaborate portico is a focal point of the Queen Street streetscape. Built originally as the seat of government for Lincoln County, it is to this day an important civic structure. It is designated under the Ontario Heritage Act, protected by an Ontario Heritage Trust easement and is also a National Historic Site. (990.5.336) **by Leah Wallace**

Painting of William Riley Home

This sketch of the log house of William Riley is the only extant image of an early home built by a former slave in the town of Niagara's "coloured village," roughly the area bounded by King, William, Ann and Butler streets. The sketch was donated to the museum by Mary Ann Guillen, Mr. Riley's daughter, who was Janet Carnochan's major source of information about the town's nineteenth century black community. The drawing was done for Mrs. Guillen by a female acquaintance, shortly before the squared timber building was pulled down in the 1880s.

William Riley, an escaped slave from Fredericksburg, Virginia, bought the one-acre town lot, 276, at the corner of Mary and Victoria streets, from William Dickson for £50 in 1819, becoming the third black man to own property in the village. The price was fair for land in the area. However, one does wonder why Mr. Dickson paid only five shillings for it a short time earlier. Neither transaction was registered until 1886.

Mr. Riley built the house in 1819, a year after his marriage at Lake Lodge (the home of Rev. Robert Addison), to Rev. Addison's German servant, Fanny. By 1851, eight family members lived in the house: William, Fanny (57), their children Mary Ann (27), Fanny (20), Edward (18) and three grandchildren, William (11), Fanny (3) and Edward (1).

After Riley's death in 1860, Edward and his sisters inherited lot 276. The last family member to own the land was William's granddaughter, Fanny Rowley, who also owned 177 King and 143 King Street, and the Rowley Block on Queen Street. She left town in 1905, ending the family's connection with lot 276.

Mrs. Guillen's lively and informative recollections about the Riley family and the larger black community can be found in Niagara Historical Society Pamphlet #2. (991.090)

by Joy Ormsby

Dress (circa 1915)

This cream-coloured dress was owned by Mrs. Evelyn Rand. It is made of embroidered net and has a pink taffeta cummerbund. It was a party dress to be worn in the afternoons and evenings, but was not a ball gown.

The Rand family was quite prominent in Town. My personal recollection of the family is their horse-drawn carriage, which took them to St. Mark's Church for Sunday service, driving past my house on King Street. I also remember that the Rands always had a July 4th celebration, to which townspeople were invited and which I attended several times. There were four Rand children, two of them girls. I remember them dressed in these short dresses towards the end of the 1920s, which was the Flapper Era.

The Rands were one of the many American families who summered in Niagara-on-the-Lake. One of the highlights of the summer season was the fireworks display that Mr. George Rand put on every July 4th. People would come to watch the dazzling show including the finale, the Stars and Strips in blazing colour. (981.25.2) **by Marianne Buyers**

View taken from Court House Niagara in 1898 for Sir Jno Bourinot's article in Canadian Magazine

1898 Photograph of the Market Square from on top of the Courthouse

What a feeling – 108 years after this photograph was taken in 1898, to look at it and recognize still-existing important Town landmarks.

At the front, to the left, is the Olde Angel Inn; at the far upper left, the spire of St Andrew's Church; and, in the centre, Grace United Church. The neighbourhood of Chautauqua appears on the far horizon, marked by the outline of the Chautauqua Hotel.

The Angel Inn, without immediate neighbours, stands as a strong, imposing building, with the roof and chimney showing years of wear. One can almost imagine the smoke curling out of the chimney, with happy revelers taking refuge – as they still do today – from the nasty weather that appears to be brewing in the distance.

This is a photograph that I would love to have in my own home as a constant reminder of how, although many things in life change, the basics remain the same. The Olde Angel Inn remains strongly rooted in the community, right in the heart of Market Square, in the same shadow of the Court House as when this image was captured in 1898.

(993.544)

by Harry Edgecombe

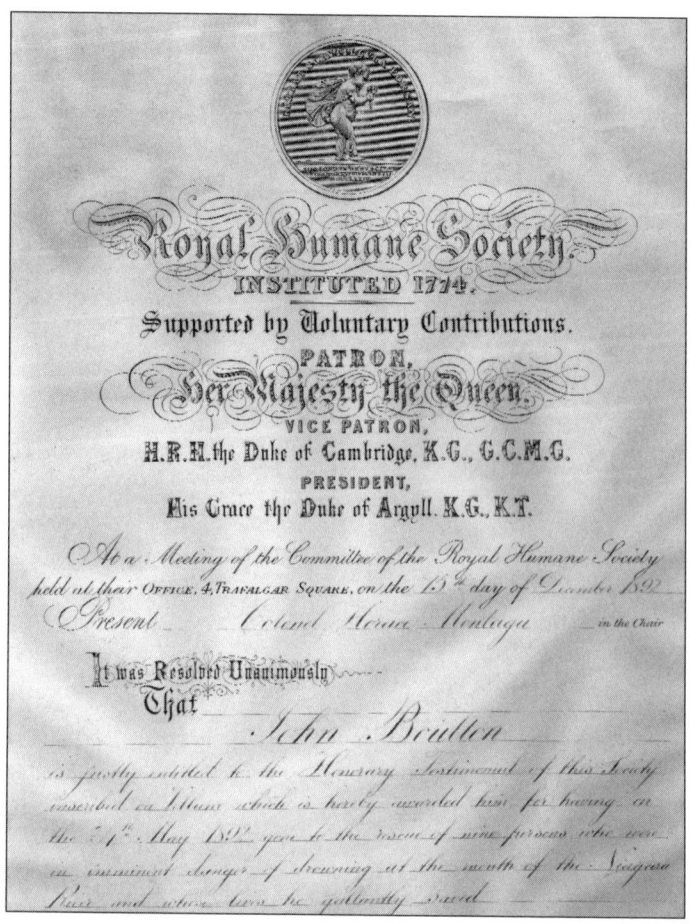

Certificate from the Royal Humane Society
May 24th, 1892 – Nine Lives Saved By Local Fishermen

On May 24th, 1892, 45 to 50 boats would have been rented to tourists from the beach area in front of the Queen's Royal Hotel.

Also available for rent was the sailboat *Katie*, winner of several local races. The Andrews brothers, their two sisters and the Averys took the *Katie* out this blustery day. The wind was blowing from the southwest, nothing dangerous if you knew the river and knew how to handle a sailboat. There was always a tricky spot opposite the Queen's Royal Hotel and as you headed up for the lake, you would run into a lull and the sails would hang limp. Then you would suddenly get a puff, dangerous if unexpected. A gust caught the party off guard and flipped the *Katie* spilling everyone into the water.

Local fisherman Jack Boulton, who had a boathouse at the foot of King Street and a row of bathing houses on his beach just up-river, saw what had happened. Jack and his helper, Bill Thornton, launched Jack's fishboat, hastened to this near tragedy and rescued everyone. Jack's official commendation, on vellum, from the Royal Humane Society was awarded for "having gone to the rescue of nine persons who were in imminent danger of drowning at the mouth of the Niagara River and whose lives he gallantly saved."

Incidentally, in all the years of fishing out of Niagara-on-the-Lake, no commercial fisherman has ever been known to lose his life while fishing. (994.5.408) **by Terry Boulton**

Minute Book Town of Niagara 1793

This interesting artefact records the actions of the civic leaders of the fledgling community of Newark from 1793 to 1842.

The first meeting was held on August 17, 1793 by virtue of an Act of the Legislature of Upper Canada. Constable William Mollyneux presided and Ralfe Clench was the clerk. At this and subsequent meetings, the town officers were appointed: clerk, assessors, collectors, town and church wardens, poundkeepers, fenceviewers and overseers of highways. All meetings were presided over by the constable.

The bylaws passed at the first meeting and reaffirmed at following meetings were few: "Hogs cannot be allowed to run at large." " The height of fences should be five feet to be lawful." In 1798 a resolution was added: "All carriages coming to the town should keep the road and all carriages coming from the town turn out for them." In 1801, "Stallion colts were not allowed to run at large after one year of age." In 1808, carriage drivers were directed to "give half the road and keep to the right hand side."

The meetings were held yearly, in March, generally in an inn. There is no record of meetings held from 1814 to 1816. In 1800 the Town is referred to as Niagara. From 1837 on, the meetings are called Township meetings.

A Board of Commissioners devised a division of labour for Township duties. Men 21 years and up had to give two days' work per year. The last two pages is a register of marks used by farmers to identify their hogs and cattle.

The lists of officers, labourers and farmers provide a valuable resource for researchers. The Minute Book shows the determination of the early "inhabitant electors" to govern themselves and gives us a deeper understanding of their way of life. (994.5.466) **by Sheila Tierney**

Picturesque Canada booklets

A publication like *Picturesque Canada* is evidence of the patriotism and respect for their history of Canadians in the later nineteenth century. In "The Niagara District" by Miss Louisa Murray we read, "These memories and associations of the brave days of old ought not to be less sacred and guarded possessions because the foes who once dyed the Niagara's crystal waters with blood are now friends and hold its joint ownership in peaceful rivalry. Through the heroic valour, sufferings and sacrifices of the men who defended Queenston Heights a nation was born, destined, we may well believe, to live as long as the famous river on whose banks the first touch of national life was felt."

The copy of *Picturesque Canada* in the Niagara Historical Museum is particularly interesting. It is in its original wrappers in 36 parts, published at 60 cents per part, for subscribers only. It is dedicated to The Marquis of Lorne, the Governor General, and Her Royal Highness, the Princess Louise, whose portraits appear on the front cover of each part. By publishing the book in parts, the publishers hoped to better manage the expenses ($110,000, according to information on the wrapper) incurred in such an expensive enterprise.

I like to read Louisa Murray's descriptions of Niagara scenes and compare them with those same scenes today. Approaching the Town from the direction of Queenston, "we pass through a grove of old oak trees, surrounded by a natural plain, or 'opening' three- quarters of a mile in extent, its grassy surface kept closely cropped by grazing cattle….This plain, always called the common, was reserved for military purposes." Apart from the cattle, very recognizable! (995.230.1-995.230.36) **by Robert Knight**

Lantern Slide of the French Thorns

Artefacts in the Museum attesting to the presence of the French in Niagara are relatively scarce, limited to trade axes and a French coin. The French undoubtedly used these axes to trade with the Natives for furs. Maps from the seventeenth and eighteenth centuries list them as items for trade. The coin, dated 1722, further tells us that sometime during the French occupation of Fort Niagara (1725-1759), a visitor came to "our" side of the river with money in his pocket. A map of Fort Niagara dated 1759, held by the Museum, even shows a garden in the area of what is now Fort George. I like to imagine an avid gardener rowing across the river to tend his cabbages.

But the most romantic story concerning the French presence has to do with a pair of thorn trees that can still be seen on the Common in the area of Fort George. Legend has it that these trees, known as the French Thorns, sprang from a branch of the tree from which Christ's crown of thorns was taken. Pope Clement brought the original branch to Italy from Jerusalem. It supplied the stock brought to Canada by the somewhat hazy figure of Count Bois le Grand, who is said to have planted two thorn trees near the Niagara River. William Kirby celebrated the thorns in "Canadian Idylls"

> Count Bois le Grand sought out a spot of loveliness…
> Hard by the sheltering grove of oak he set the holy thorn
> Where still it grows and ever shows
> How sharp the crown of thorn Christ wore for man

The photograph dates from the early twentieth century. These gnarled trees still grow on the river side of Queen's Parade. They provide an intriguing link to the French presence in Niagara, and may add interest to your walk by the Common. (996.033E)

by Diane Debenham

German Gas Mask

"The bunk was the top of a great box in which were five German caps with badges, two spike helmets and belts. We divided the souvenirs and went back to the upstairs"
—Will Bird, France, 1918

The Second Battle of Ypres, fought in the spring of 1915, introduced Allied soldiers to the terror of chlorine gas. The technological innovations that followed meant that soldiers would have to struggle against an ever-increasing arsenal of chemical weapons. It was in this environment that the first gas masks were produced.

Featured is a German World War I Model 1917 mask, composed of an all-leather face piece, glass lenses, and rubber and cloth straps running along the back; ensuring a somewhat secure fit. The chemical filter is directly attached, differentiating it from the Allied "small box respirator" mask where the filter was carried in a satchel, worn on the back and away from the face. The German approach made the mask less cumbersome, but reduced the soldier's ability to accurately fire his weapon. Respirators on the mask wore out faster than in Allied models, and the leather sections, used due to economic shortages, often failed under high concentrations of gas.

It is likely that this mask made its way to Canada as part of a collection of war souvenirs, high-demand trophies collected from the conflict. Soldiers searched for weapons, clothing, and equipment to bring back as mementos of their actions overseas. Nearly 100 years later, souvenirs such as this one still serve as reminders of that great conflict. (FA69.1119)

by Sarah Cozzi

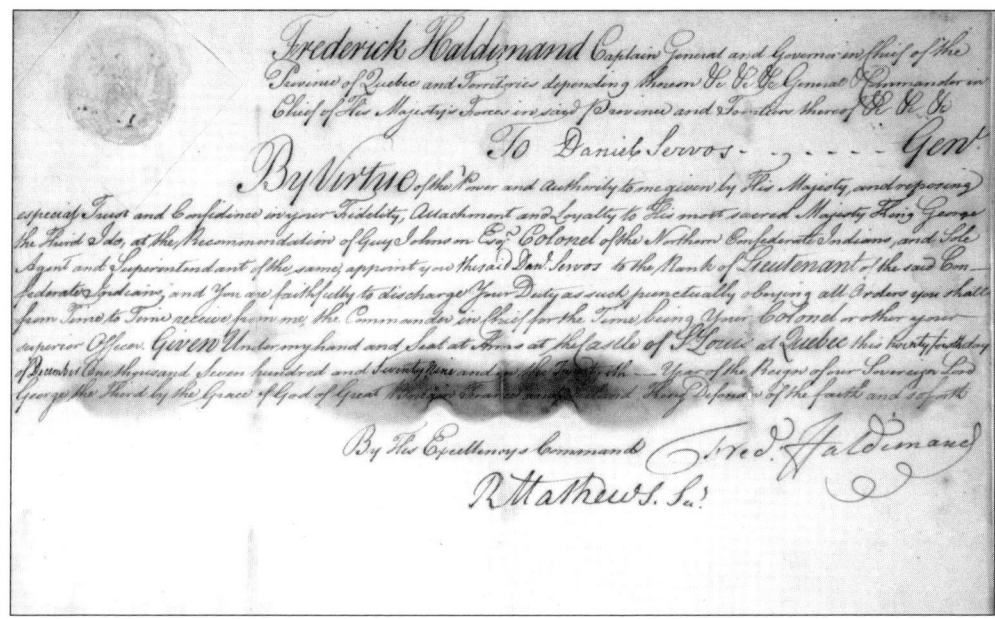

Certificate of Appointment for Daniel Servos

"Why are we going to Palatine Hill?" It's 1940; I'm eleven. We're driving near Virgil where we lived in the 1920s. "Because you'll see and hear some real history."

It was a rainy day – no chance of running around outside. The old frame house depressed me – run down, paint needed. The door was opened by an old, friendly but serious lady. "Gloomy" best describes the interior. Mary Servos had been an interesting neighbour for my parents. The adult chatter was meaningless for me. My orders were to "sit quietly."

The adjoining room was filled with dusty old furniture, implements and wooden or leather chests. From them Mary Servos removed old military uniforms and swords. She talked about her ancestors and their exploits (including Laura Secord's historic walk).

Old certificates on the walls told of military, citizenship and property histories. Reading them was difficult – they were faded, torn, stained. One especially fascinated me – 1779, naming Daniel Servos, Lieutenant of Confederate Indians.

History started to come alive! Here I was in a pre-1800 house with an 80-year-old describing events before Canada, Ontario, Niagara-on-the-Lake or even the U.S.A. (the Natives were vital British allies during the 1780s War of Independence) existed.

Leaving Palatine Hill, I know a seed of historical awareness had been planted in me. History wasn't just dates, wars and facts. It meant real people with rich stories to tell. Laura Secord ceased to be just a picture on a box of my mother's favourite chocolates.

(FA69.3.152) **by Donald L. King**

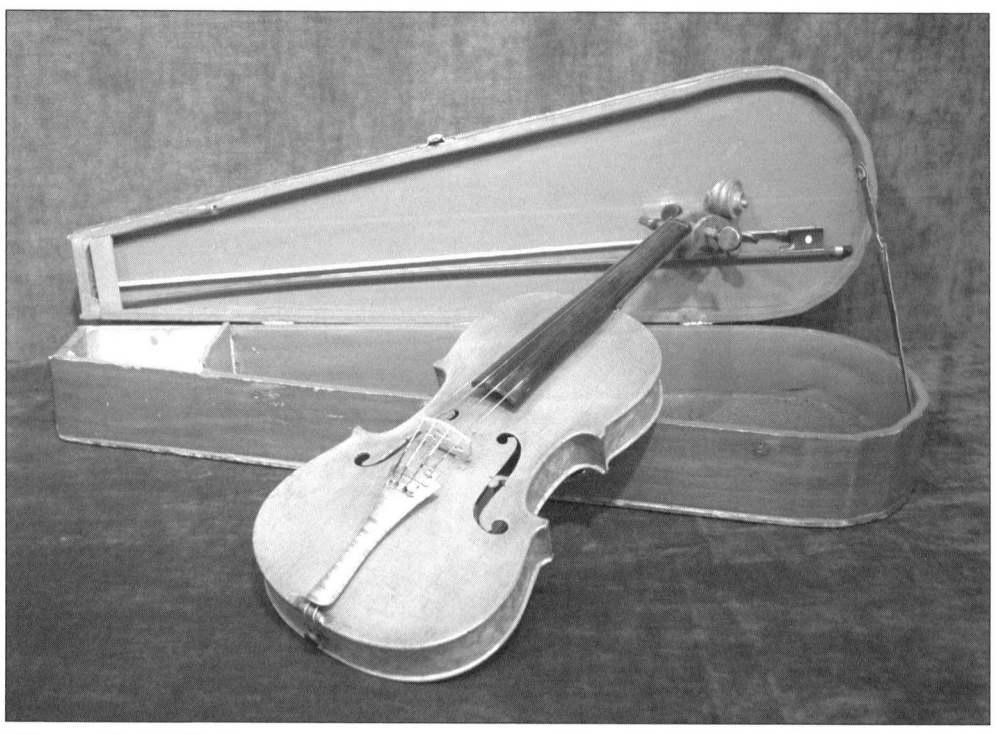

Hiram Field Violin

This violin was hand made of tiger maple by Hiram Field (1833 – 1923). Hiram was a descendant of the Field family that built the first brick house on River Road in Niagara. The violin is stamped "H. Field 1896", and it is one of approximately 12 violins that were made by him. Hiram was a bachelor all his life, and he farmed in the Laurel area near present-day Orangeville. He carved violins and other wooden objects in his spare time. When Hiram passed away in 1923, his nephew Nelson Field inherited all of his violins. The donor of this artefact, Mrs. Ellen Donald, is also related to the Field family, and she recalled visiting the home of Nelson Field, where her father purchased one of the violins. In 2005 Ellen decided to donate the violin to the Niagara Historical Museum, and I remember travelling to Mrs. Donald's house in Simcoe, Ontario to pick up the instrument. I spent a very pleasant afternoon with Ellen and Bill Donald, talking about the history surrounding Hiram Field and his violins.

Mrs. Donald also owns a lovely maple spoon carved by Hiram, and another person has located a beautifully carved maple cane with an inscription on the handle that reads "H. Field, Laurel, 1898." Perhaps more of talented Hiram Field's carvings will be discovered in the future. (2005.014.001) **by Monica Taylor**

Servos Mill Branding Iron

Wording on this branding iron reads: "J Servos 196 lbs. U. Canada." Its dimensions are 64.5cm (handle), and 11.4 x 7 x 3.2cm (circular branding head).

Among the many tools used in the Servos grist mills (c.1783–1911), one of the largest is a branding iron used to mark the heads of wooden flour barrels to validate the weight, miller's name and mill location. Loyalists brought many tools with them from the United States but the Servos branding iron was made by an Upper Canada blacksmith. There were three Servos grist/flour mills, all merchant mills selling mainly to the British army. The first was built by the King in 1783 on Four Mile Creek. It was operated by a retired soldier, Daniel Servos, from the Mohawk Valley. The mill was burned during the War of 1812, and burned again by accident in 1820. Rebuilt again in the same location, it continued operating until 1906, finally collapsing in 1911.

The first Upper Canada Flour Inspection Laws required every miller selling flour to brand his barrels with the name of the mill that packed the flour and the initials "U.C." with the net weight of flour to be 196 pounds.

The branding iron miller "J Servos" is John Dease Servos, 1784–1847. We know he was subject to the 1820 Upper Canada Flour Inspection Laws and the branding iron would not meet the much larger dimension requirements of the 1841 Laws. The branding iron was therefore used at the Servos mill during the period 1820–1841 when the miller was John Dease Servos. (FA69.3.197)

by Robert Miller

Parliament Chair

Three chairs in the Museum's collection are a visual bond with early Niagara and the time when this was the Capital of Upper Canada.

The first is a handsome Windsor chair, with arms, with seven splats over eleven. It is reputed to be one of the chairs used in the first Provincial Legislature. It was preserved by the Servos family and so its provenance is certain. Its design and condition confirm its suitability for use in the first Legislature, in contrast to local chairs, which were mainly ladder backed with rush seats. The seat of this chair has a saddle shape and measures 36 cm in depth. The construction is called "hole and wedge" as holes were drilled and posts inserted with the wedge to tighten the splats and rungs. The feet were splayed for strength and balance and the legs are supported with the traditional H-brace.

The second chair is also of superior quality, although it does not have the same provenance. It is more likely early nineteenth century and because of the more detailed turning and shape may have been imported. It is a Windsor design and shows how middle to upper class homes were furnished in the early 1800s. The chair has seven splats and the same "hole and wedge" construction, although the seat is slightly narrower. It also came from the Servos collection.

The third (pictured) chair probably comes from the First Legislature. It is an armchair with curved back slats arranged in reverse pairs. It is a popular French Canadian design. The chair has a historical connection to Alexander Stewart who was a member of that Legislature.

Looking at these chairs, one can imagine being seated in them trying to resolve the perplexing problems that confronted Lieutenant-Governor Simcoe and the early settlers of this new country. (FA69.3.236.1 - FA69.3.236.4 & 970.563)

by Cam Calder

Dispatch Case of the Honourable William Claus — *family connection*

Red leather 'Muckleston Patent' 1812 c dispatch case, 38.5 x 27.5 cm, brass lock and clips on outside. Inside are two pockets and a box at the bottom. Smaller blue pocket inside one pocket. Loaned to the Honourable William Claus 1765-1826. Born, New York of a prominent Empire Royalist family he married well.
1787-Lieutenant-60th Foot Regiment of the British Army.
1795-Promoted to Captain.
Appointments and promotions:-
1796-Settled in NOTL, Deputy Superintendent of Indian Department responsible for Six Nations of Grand River at Fort George. Adamant and argumentative that Native lands were to be sold through the crown.
1797-Trustee for Six Nations of Grand River, in particular the Ojibwa.
1800-Deputy Superintendent General for Upper Canada.
1802-Lieutenant county of Oxford, incorporating Militia.
1803-Justice of the Peace, Trustee Niagara Public School, Commissioner of Customs Niagara District.
1807-Commenced realigning British Government with Chiefs of Six Nations against Americans.
1812-Appointed to Legislative Council. When war with America, Colonel 1st Lincoln Militia and Flank Commander of British Regulars at Fort George-Queenston Heights, when loaned despatch case.
1816-Appointed to prestigious Executive Council, negotiating division of customs duties with Lower Canada.
Obtained from British Government 500 p.s. towards restoring St. Marks Church.
1820-Negotiated agreements in Toronto with assurances to Mississauga Ojibwa.
Wrote 'The Origin Of The Many Ceremonies and Customs Among The Indians'
His immaculate records of flowers, vegetable gardens and orchards provide an insight into horticulture in Niagara.
1826-November 11 died. (971.169)

by Anthony J. Griffiths

The Gonder Family Table

When the landmark antique volumes The *Furniture of Old Ontario* and *The Heritage of Upper Canadian Furniture* appeared in the 1970s, it was not surprising to discover that the oldest table featured in both books had a Niagara connection. The table is the Gonder family table (c.1750) in the collection of the Niagara Historical Museum. Both authors suggested it was brought to Niagara from Pennsylvania. Their interpretation of its origins was based upon the form, or style of the flat box stretcher base, which was a popular attribute of tables before the 1780s, the period of Loyalist settlement. The following discussion questions this and demonstrates the possibility of an early Niagara origin.

The assumption that the table style is too early to have been made in Niagara, demonstrates a general lack of awareness of Euro-Canadian settlement in Niagara, which began before other parts of the province. The first ship to sail the upper Great Lakes, the *Griffin*, was built in Niagara as early as 1679. Initially French, subsequently English speaking occupants settled this area, including all the garrisons along the Niagara River. Loyalist refugees took up land on the west bank as early as 1781. They brought with them their belongings, including furnishings like this table.

Another point of consideration is the material of construction used in the composition of the table. It is generally accepted that Ontario joiners crafted furniture with pine as a secondary wood. Their counterparts in Pennsylvania and New York generally preferred tulipwood or poplar as the secondary material. While the principal wood of the Gonder table is a black walnut, available in all parts of these locations, its secondary wood is indeed pine. The Gonder family have left few records, but it is clear that they lived in the Black Creek area of the Niagara Peninsula. They were reputed to be Pennsylvania *Deutsch*, and the pegtop form of this table was commonly found among the Germanic people. Their home is said to have been a command post of Sir Gordon Drummond during the siege of Fort Erie and the table used by him. British officers were accustomed to traveling with large amounts of baggage and furnishings and often sold their possessions by auction upon moving to a new post. Consequently many of these pieces found their way to local homes, which may account for the provenance of this table.

The true story of the origins of the Gonder family table remains an untold secret of history. While it is possible that this great piece of Canadiana may have been wrought in a Niagara shop or elsewhere, it has, in fact, enjoyed a long life and history in Niagara. (970.681)

by Jon K. Jouppien

Railway Car Builder's Stencil

Railway car builders, like Brainerd Pearson & Company, formerly of Niagara-on-the-Lake, stencilled their names on cars they constructed as a normal practice of car builder identification. This is a copper stencil, 35 by 24cm and 5 mm thick with cut out 2.5 cm high letters, used for that purpose. There are paint speckles on it, indicating that this stencil was actually used in service, and not a spare.

The Niagara Car Works were an "on-line" customer of the Erie and Ontario Railway (later the Canada Southern) in the mid1800s. On-line means they had a direct physical connection to the railway via a siding. They were located on Niagara Harbour and Dock Company land at the instigation of Samuel Zimmerman, after he bought the failed dock company in the fall of 1853. He leased the building to Messres. A.H. Brainerd, C.O. Pierson & R.G. Benedict. Brainerd managed the railway car manufacturing operation until he retired in February 1856, at which time the company was reorganized as Messres. Pierson and Benedict. The copper stencil therefore dates to 1854-55, probably 1855 when the car factory buildings were destroyed in the great Niagara tornado.

The Brainerds, who were involved in the original partnership that formed the Niagara Car Works, were Alexander Hamilton Brainerd and his younger brother, George Washington Brainerd. Both were born in Niagara County, New York, but later moved to Rome, New York, when their family relocated there in the 1820s, after their father accepted a contract on the Erie Canal. Alexander H. Brainerd later became a railway contractor and served for a time as superintendent of the Champlain & St. Lawrence Railroad at Montreal, before becoming managing partner of the Niagara Car Works. He retired in early 1856 and returned to Rome after his wife died later in April.

The Merrilees Collection and a CNR Passenger Equipment book show two first class passenger cars – Grand Trunk Railway (GTR) 83 and 84 – as being built by the Niagara Car Works in 1859. Merrilees also claim that 302 box cars were built by the same company for the GTR between 1858 and 1861. It is not known whether the other large railway concern in Southern Ontario, the Great Western Railway, ever had any cars built by The Niagara Car Works, or exactly how long the company was building railway cars.

(2001.225) **by Andrew Panko**

Queen's Royal Hotel Ledger Books, 17 in the collection

The Queen's Royal Hotel stood in what is now Queen's Royal Park from 1869 until 1929, when it was torn down.

It's hard to imagine now how grand and world-renowned a hotel it was. The hotel itself was four storeys high, painted white with green shutters, and its grounds ran from where the gazebo is now to the back of the Niagara-on-the-Lake Golf Club. Visitors from all over the world arrived by steamer and train, drawn by international tennis tournaments, two golf courses, grand verandahs and a casino/dance hall that projected out over the mouth of the river.

A photo of ten, very young bellhops reveals a few still-familiar town names. Dance cards show John Philip de Souza played in the dance hall. Miss Gertrude Eckersley (a Vassar graduate) and her sister held their "coming out" parties there. The bar book shows the tabs of the regular customers; who paid regularly and how often they drank. There is a photo of the Duke of York (later King George V) and the Duchess (later Queen Mary) who visited Niagara in 1901 and stayed at the Queen's Royal Hotel, only to be made to sit on the verandah until 3am as the hotel's newly installed acetylene gas light fixtures leaked. They were not amused.

by Shelagh Wallace

REPORT OF THE OPENING OF MEMORIAL HALL
JUNE 4th, 1907
(Abridged)
Published in 1908
By Janet Carnochan (pictured)

Society & Museum Founder Janet Carnochan

It has been suggested by several members that the next publication of our Society should be a report of the opening of our building and that this should contain, as far as possible, the addresses given, the list of Contributors to the Building Fund, the items of expense in the construction and furnishing and some account of the most interesting articles in the collection. It is to be regretted however, that some of the addresses could not be obtained, being impromptu and not fully reported.

To begin at the beginning of the Evolution of the Building, but how to reach by any method the beginning of anything, the environment of each person concerned, the circumstances which culminated in certain work done, all the thoughts maturing in many minds and at last crystallized into action. It is never possible to gather these together as the drops of all the tiny streamlets which trickle down uniting in the full grown river.

To begin at the beginning of the first public act which led ultimately to the erection of our Historical Building some reference must be made to the foundation of our Society. An article was sent to the local paper urging the formation of an Historical Society and shortly after, the following invitation appeared:

"A Meeting will be held in the Public Library on Thursday evening, December 12th, 1895, at 7:30 p.m. to take steps to organize an Historical Society for Niagara. A cordial invitation is given to all interested in the subject to be present." At the meeting Mr. Henry Paffard was called on to act as Chairman and Mr. R.C. Burns as Secretary. It was decided to form a Society and the following officers were elected: Wm. Kirby, Patron; Miss Carnochan, President; H. Paffard, Vice-President; Alfred Ball, Secretary; Mrs. Alexander Servos, Treasurer; Committee, Rev. J.C. Garrett, Wm. Seymour, B.A., W.R. McClelland and John D. Servos.

Besides the officials appointed, there were present Russell Wilkinson, Wm. Harrison, R.C. Burns, Mrs. B. Nash, and the Misses Winterbottom, Baxter and Clement. The Rev. Dr. Scadding and Canon Bull were elected Honorary Members. A Committee was appointed to draft a Constitution and By-Laws before next meeting.

An application to the Town Council was sent, and the Grand Jury Room in the third story of the Court House was granted for Meetings and to form an Historical Collection. It was decided that the Anniversary day should be 17th September, to celebrate the Meeting of the Parliament of Upper Canada at Niagara, then Newark, in 1792, and that the Annual

Meeting should be on the 13th October to commemorate the Battle of Queenston Heights, 1812.

The card of membership gives the motto: "The Love of Country Guides" and states that "the objects of the Society are the encouragement of the study of Canadian History and Literature, the collection and safe preservation of Canadian Historical Records and Relics and the building up of Canadian Loyalty and Patriotism."

Each member is asked to give or loan to the Society, documents or relics to add to the collection in the Historical Room or aid in any other way the aims of the Society."

The First Anniversary was held in the Town Park in 1896, the speakers and others were entertained at lunch at Long's Hotel and there was an Historical Exhibit in Rowley's block in the charge of John D. Servos to whose zeal is collecting, the utmost praise was due. The Speakers were: Rev. Canon Bull, Capt. Cruickshank (now Colonel), Mrs. Curzon, Miss FitzGibbon, Col. J.G. Currie, Jas. Hiscott, M.P.P., and Wm. Kirby, F.R.S.C. The Band of the 39th Battalion was kindly furnished by Col. Otter, the Military Camp being held at that time, and the High School Glee Club sang, led by Wm. Seymour, B.A. After lunch, St. Mark's Graveyard had been visited and many graves decorated.

It is not intended to give the history of the Society during the ten years since. The work went on regularly and the room was found too small to contain the articles but as the next steps are referred to in a paper read June 4th, these need not be repeated. A Committee was formed to arrange for the important day of the opening. Mr. Chas. Hunter kindly offered to entertain the Lieutenant-Governor, whose presence we were fortunate enough to secure.

Mrs. Chas. Hunter, Manager of the Standard Life Assurance Co., and Mrs. Hunter entertained at their beautiful summer home, the Lt.-Governor, Major Macdonald, Mrs. Macdonald, Rev. J.C. Garrett, Mrs. J.C. Garrett and A.H.U. Colquhoun, while others were entertained by the Society at Doyle's Hotel. The visitors were met at the boat by the President of the Society, Mr. Eckersley, and W.J. Wright, M.A. Among those entertained were Dr. Bain, C.C. James, Rev. N. Smith, Miss Gilkison, Brantford and other friends.

Among those who were present and registered were His Honor, Sir Mortimer Clark attended by his official Secretary, Major McDonald, Dr. Bain, Chief Librarian, Dr. A.H.U. Colquhoun, Dep. Minister of Education, C.C. James, F.R.S.C., Dep. Minister of Agriculture, Mrs. J.F. Macdonald, Chas. Hunter, Mrs. Chas. Hunter, Rev. N. Smith, Mrs. H. Thompson, Rev. A.B. Sherk, Mrs. Miller, Miss Gray, T.M. Rowland, Mrs. Rowland, Mrs. Wilson, Miss Lawler, Mrs. Collins all of Toronto. Johnson Clench, Mrs. J.G. Currie, Dr. Jessop, M.P.P., R. Walker, C.A. Case, Mrs. Bixby, C.A. Wilson, A.R. Carnochan, Mrs. Clench of St. Catharines, Col. Cruickshank, F.R.S.C., Dr. and Mrs. Walker, C.A. Foulger, W.P. Gonder, F.H. Leslie, Mrs. Birdsall of Niagara Falls, Mrs. Gilkinson, Brantford, Miss Gonder and Miss Durham, Black Creek, R.G. Davis, London, Miss McKay, Mimico, Mrs. Walker, Buffalo, Mrs. Walker, Glencoe, F.J. Arline, St. Thomas, J.M. Field, W. Crouch, Miss Crouch, Virgil, Mrs. Scott, Cincinnati, Mrs. Row, Cleveland, Mrs. McPherson, Ottawa, Mrs. F. Anderson, Chicago, Miss Fairbairn, Weston, Rev. J.C. Garrett, Mrs. Garrett, Rev. A. F. MacGregor, Rev. P.J. Bench, Major Hiscott, Dr. Anderson, Chas. A.F. Ball, Mrs. Ball, Mrs. Wood, Miss Joanna E. Wood, Mrs. McGaw, Miss Alma, Miss Winterbottom, J. de W. Randall, T.F. Best, J. Bottomley, Mrs. A. Servos, W.J. Wright, M.A., Mrs. Bottomley, J.H. Burns, Mrs. J.H. Burns, Miss Beavan, F. Winthrop, C. Thonger, W.S. Lansing, Mrs. Lansing, A.W. Wright, Jos. Walker, H. Ruthven, Mrs. Jno. Carnochan, W.E. Lyall, F. J. Rowland, Mrs. Rowland, Miss Anderson, Miss M. Ball, Miss M. Servos, W.R. McClelland,

Miss Follett, Miss Bernard, P. Librock, J.A. Black, Mrs. Geddes, Mrs. Billings and many others. Besides these, the Press was well represented as there were Reporters here from the *Toronto Globe, News, Star and Telegram*, also *St. Catharines Standard* and *Niagara Falls Review*. It had been decided that the speaking should be in a large marquee tent as on account of the number of upright cases in the room, it was not adapted for a large crowd; a smaller tent was provided for refreshments, but as on account of the rain, the attendance was less than expected, it was decided that the speaking should be in the Building and that afterwards refreshments should be served to all present in the large tent.

On a platform covered with rich rugs kindly provided by Mrs. Miles, were seated the Lieutenant-Governor, the President and Vice-President of the Society. The room was brilliant with flags and fragrant with flowers and altogether with the array in the cases of military accoutrements, pictures, flags, and flowers, a fine "TOUT ENSEMBLE" was presented. A handsome palm, sent by the Niagara Navigation Company was conspicuous.

The opening prayer as made by the Rev. J.C. Garrett, the Vice-President, after which His Honor, Sir Mortimer Clark, made an address first congratulating the Society on the Building and its contents and briefly reviewed the events of the last fifty years in Canada, showing how a feeling of loyalty had been developed and fostered by the events of the War of 1812, the Trent affair, and the Boer War, thus binding together Canada and the Mother Country. He emphasized the importance of historical societies and the value to the young of such an object lesson as the contents of this room would be. He spoke of the changes he had seen since coming to the Country in 1859 and of the greater interest in historical research and of the stronger feeling of patriotism a new spirit seemed to control the people of today and we were living in the midst of the awaking of a new life. Newcomers not understanding our government and knowing little of Canadian history were apt to overlook the work of those who had brought about the present condition of a settled country and people who were loyal subjects of the British Empire. Niagara was the Mecca for Tourists. The Niagara Peninsula had been made sacred by the blood of those who fought and died, whose brave deeds are an inspiration to all and who should be honored by all.

The three places of greatest historic interest in Canada were Louisburg, Quebec and Niagara. Young people should be brought to Memorial Hall and there taught the history of their forefathers and that Canada was part of a great Empire. Imperialism spread the knowledge of British law, which stood for civil liberty. An Imperialist was not one who was always "begging some one to tread on the tail of his coat." It was important to preserve all links with the past that the young should be brought in touch with it. The Lieutenant-Governor then declared the building open.

In spite of the rain every one seemed happy and pleased. Many stayed in the room taking their refreshments and in examining more closely the collection consisting of Military Clothing, Weapons, Documents, Portraits of Early Inhabitants, early Niagara Printing, Rare Books and Pamphlets, Women's Work, Clothing, Churches, Household Articles grouped round an old Mantel, Old China, Early Boats, Indian remains, Pictures, old Furniture Papers, Autographs, Deeds, Scrap Books, Miscellaneous.

The Evening Meeting was held in the Town Hall and was presided over by Rev. J.C. Garrett. In spite of the pouring rain, the room was full to the doors. The Programme was carried out completely with the exception of one Speaker, Hon. Peter Porter of Niagara Falls, New York, whose letter explained that the serious illness of his son prevented him coming. His absence was a great disappointment as his rousing speech two years ago was remembered. It is to be regretted that the address of Col. Cruickshank, F.R.C.S.C. cannot be given in full as it was spoken not written.

It was strongly patriotic in the tone and referred briefly to the different features of the Military History of Niagara from the first settlement, during and after the Revolutionary War, through the different invasions of our Territory in the War of 1812, showing how the men, women and even the children had helped in defending their country.

The eminent historian of the Niagara Peninsula than whom no one has equal knowledge on the subject, was listened to with great attention as his well known thoroughness, impartiality and powers of research are acknowledged by all and command respect. A song followed, by the High School Glee Club, led by Miss Anderson, one of the Teachers, "Canada". Then followed a paper by C.C. James, F.R.S.C., Deputy Minister of Agriculture on the Early Legislators of Niagara which was replete with much curious and interesting historic lore. This paper we are happy to be able to give in full. The audience was then delighted with the song "Canada", (which may become the Canadian Anthem) by Col. Galloway which was so heartily encored that another patriotic song was given by "John Bull."

Then following "The Evolution of Our Historical Building" by the President, and this by special request is also given in full. The Glee Club gave another song, "Canada, God and Our Land." The members of the Glee Club were the Misses L. Carnochan, L. Hartley, E. Redhead, C. Eckersley, H. Gordon, F. Lee, H. Stevens, N. Irvine, E. Doherty, M. Lynch, W. Taylor, the pianist being Miss May Burns. The meeting was closed with "God Save The King."

Memorial Hall, May 2007

THE EVOLUTION OF OUR HISTORICAL BUILDING
Published in 1908
By Janet Carnochan

Since this, we believe is the first building erected in the Province for purely historical purposes, it may be worth while to follow out the steps taken in its inception, planning, providing funds, construction and now we hope to say, its happy conclusion. When our Society was formed in Dec., 1895, the idea of an historical collection soon occurred to us and a room which is itself an historic room having been that of the Grand Jury was granted us by the Town Council in the Third Storey of the Court House, a long narrow room and however contracted its dimensions or however difficult of access, still we were thankful to have a room and here we started our collection in the Spring of 1896, the September Loan Exhibit being very helpful to us and gradually articles flowed in till our room was crowded, the wall covered with pictures and every available corner filled.

During the summers 1905, 1906, permission was granted by the Town council to use the Town Hall, with the proviso that we must return to our own room in September, as the Town Hall would then be required for the Town and Township Fair. It may be imagined that the labour of moving was no slight thing and this has been done five times, twice in 1905, twice in 1906 and our final move in February, 1907, and all with very little expense and with little breakage or loss. It may be imagined that the formation of an Historical Society, an historical collection, and the erection of a building met with cold indifference, indeed with copious showers of cold water from many, but on the other hand we have always had a number of faithful members and constant friends whose sympathy and active help have encouraged us. A word or two as to the formation of our Society I may say, that being a member first, of the Lundy's Lane Historical Society, the example set by Canon Bull and the work done by that society were all powerful factors, indeed an inspiration in forming the dream of a similar society in Niagara. A few lines were inserted in our local paper asking those interested in such an object to meet in the Library on the evening of Dec. 12, 1895. Fifteen persons assembled and I had fully formed in my mind that Rev. J.C. Garrett should be our President, but to my astonishment and indeed dismay, I was appointed to the office and have tried to discharge its duties ever since. One thing greatly in our favour has been the fact that we had had the same Secretary, active and faithful through all these years and an efficient Secretary is a great support to any Society. Also we have had only two Treasurers and these have given earnest work, the same Vice-President, Henry Paffard, and our present Vice-President J.C. Garrett, has been on the committee since the formation of the Society. A constitution was framed and very few changes have been made on it.

We began with ten members; we now have 140; we have printed fifteen pamphlets, placed eight markers on historical spots, gathered over three thousand articles, collected money for this building which with its furniture, and additions to be made will cost in the neighbourhood of $5,000.00. We now owe three hundred and fifty dollars but have faith that the liberality of our friends is not as yet exhausted. The first printed reference to a building was in a circular issued by our Society in 1898. Five hundred copies were sent out but I am sorry to say with little result, but little by little, step by step, the main idea expressed in that circular has been carried out. The opening words were: "Three years ago, Canon Bull suggested in his report, the placing of a cairn or monument of some kind to commemorate the landing of the United Empire Loyalists on our shores." Since then, at a Meeting of the Provincial Historical Association here in June, 1896, the proposition of the Niagara Historical Society in regard to this met with much approval and a grant of $50.00 was given as the nucleus of the fun, from the surplus in the hand of the Association given by the Government at the Centennial of Upper Canada, July, 1892.

This was only to be given to us when we had started the work and as a matter of fact, it only came into our hands in 1904. In the circular sent out in 1898, the closing words give the first idea of a building thus: "A late suggestion made is that in view of the increasing contents of the Historical Room (so many of those relating to the early settlers) the memorial take the form of a building for the historical collection."

Meanwhile, as our cases were overflowing two difficulties stared us in the face, 1st where to find space in the long narrow room for the articles given, it being impossible to classify them as we wished. 2nd was it safe to keep such valuable material of which it would be impossible to replace if destroyed in the third storey where it would be difficult to save anything in case of fire.

The next step was in the form of letters from the President of the Society to the Cabinet Ministers of the Province in the year 1899. The replies to these were of the usual nature of careful and cautious Ministers of the Crown, "the matter would receive their very serious consideration," "they would bring the matter before their colleagues," etc. but the letter of Hon. G.W. Ross was an encouraging one and gave the hint of what became our future action he said "a shaft or monument would cost but a small sum. However, I think your larger scheme of a fire-proof building for the safe deposit of your collection would be decidedly better and I would cheerfully lend my aid for the accomplishment of that object. If a considerable sum were contributed by yourselves it would be an inducement to us to add something to make your contribution more effective."

The next important step was taken on the 17th September, 1903, when a public meeting was called in the Court Room and different friends were invited to be with us from Toronto. A Globe Reporter, Mr. McLean was present and a very pleasant meeting resulted, A. N. Wright acted as Chairman and C.C. James, David Boyle, Rev. A. Sherk, Wm. Kirby, Mayor Jas. Aikens and Mrs. Thompson spoke. Mr. James and Mr. Boyle both strongly advised that instead of appealing to the Government, municipality or any other public organization that we began with ourselves as a Society, our townspeople and then appeal to other sources. A Committee was formed consisting of C.C. James, John Ross Robertson, Dr. Withrow, D. Boyle, Mrs. Thompson, Toronto, and in Town,

Alfred Ball, Alexander Servos, H. Paffard, R.E. Denison, F.J. Rowland, the Mayor, and the president of the Society was named convenor of the Committee. At the first meeting, a circular was presented and sent to the Toronto members for approval, five hundred copies were printed and distributed. It was decided these should be sent with a personal letter to all members at a distance to former residents of our Town and others likely to help and that a canvass of the Town should be made by the President and Treasurer of the Society following the sending out of the circular. We had to begin with $150.00 granted from the funds of the Society, the hope of the $50 held in trust for us by the O.H.S. and a member promised $50. The President undertook to write most of the letters to accompany the circulars and commenced by writing six letters each evening, for some time this was continued, afterwards four were written each evening and finally a larger or smaller number as circumstances allowed. It may be said that the members in town in general responded heartily as well as the non-members, only a few refusals were met with. The waiting for answers and their receipt was the important event of the day and its exciting feature and when for a time the letter writing ceased it seemed that everything was stale, flat and unprofitable and that something had been taken out of our life. "The Post's Arrival in the Village" so graphically described by the Poet was nothing to this. The varying replies, the failure to reply at all, the kind answers of some, the curt ones of a few, the large donations sometimes from unexpected sources, the smaller ones from people who might be expected to give large amounts all formed an interesting feature of life in the year 1904-5. These letters have been preserved and will be bound as the property of the Society.

It should have been stated before that just as our circulars were being printed a proposal was brought forward that the Town Hall on the payment of $1,000 to enable them to improve the Court Room, this was strongly urged by three of our members and very unwillingly agreed to by myself to whom as to many others the idea of a separate building. To these the way is now open for the liberality first thought of. However from special circumstances and difficulties which arose unexpectedly no steps were taken to carry out the plan of using the Town Hall and altering the Court Room. When the Spring of 1904 was reached it was determined to ask assistance from the Provincial Government. While in Toronto, a letter asked an interview with the Premier who was also the Treasurer, the answer appointing the day and hour only arrived two hours before the time fixed and the street cars taken to gather the delegations were numerous and when it was found that this very hour was also that appointed for the Premier to meet a delegation of hundreds of college graduates asking for a large grant for the University the dismay felt may be imagined, however a five minute interview was granted and the promise of the Premier made in 1899 was recalled that if we helped ourselves, help might be given, then came the quick question. "And have you done so?" "Yes, we have now $1,000." No absolute promise was given but that of looking into the matter and when some time after the supplementary list came out it was found to our satisfaction that $500.00 was given to us and now larger views dawned on us and the idea of a separate building was determined on. Many friends in Toronto helped us liberally on personal solicitation and the next spring a visit was paid to the Dominion Parliament to ask for a grant of $l,000. The object now was to show them we were not local nor even merely provincial in our aims but that we had members in different parts of the Dominion, articles in our collection from distant points, that we exchanged publications with different States and Provinces.

An interview was kindly arranged for, when almost despaired of, at nine in the evening of the last day, but one of Parliament with Hon. C.S. Hyman, the Minister of Public Works and when it was found that we now on hand had $2,000.00 dollars, a hope was extended that our prayer would be granted and when the supplementary list appeared our hearts were gladdened with the grant of $1,000.00 to be paid when the work was well under way. We now called a meeting of the whole of our members by printed post card, and in August 17th, 1905, we met to discuss the plan for a building, of which the celebrated young sculptor, Mr. Allward, gave us the first idea. We decided on certain salient features, the size, the material, the gallery, the portico, and then the plan was taken to the architect, W.B. Allan, St. Catharines, who made out specifications and drew a new plan, which, at a Committee Meeting, we approved of with certain alterations. Meanwhile, an interview was obtained with the present Premier Hon. J.S. Whitney, but that year we were informed "there was a deficit" no definite promise was given of assistance, but in April, 1906, an interview was granted with Hon. S. Whitney and Hon. A.J. Matheson, and a kind and courteous promise was given of further assistance.

It may be wondered at that we had the audacity to ask assistance from two Premiers of two different political views but the result showed that in this case, politics did not enter into historical matters for when the supplementary estimates were published a grant of $500.00 appeared. Our committee had already called for tenders by advertising in the St. Catharines and Niagara papers and in January, 1906, four tenders were received, but all far beyond our means, all reaching the sum of $7,000.00. This certainly gave us pause. Again the committee met and revised the specifications trying to eliminate the most expensive features and still cause little alteration in the appearance or solidity of the structure.

Again we advertised and this time only one tender was received and this for slightly under four thousand dollars by Messrs. Carnochan and Doritty, and this was accepted on February 10, 1906, the work to be finished in September.

A very important matter has been to referred to: viz. the obtaining a site for the building and this was almost as difficult as the selecting a site for Toronto Reference Library, although it did not drag on through years as did the decision for the Toronto building. First the town promised a site and at a joint meeting of a committee from members of the Society and the Town Council the grant of a site in the Town Park was recommended and afterwards confirmed by the Council, but an editorial in the local paper opposed this and others joining in the cry, there being talk of the resolution being rescinded, we, not wishing to antagonize public feeling did not press the matter and the next meeting of the Society when some were despairing of a spot on which to rest the sole of our foot, the president offered to present a site on Main Street, nearly opposite the R.C. Church. This was accepted but afterwards when examination showed that being on sloping ground additional expense would be incurred, an offer was made by the President's brother to exchange the present site for the first one offered and this was agreed upon by the Committee and confirmed at the Meeting of the Society. Another cry of opposition was raised that "it was so far away," "that it should be on the main street", but it is generally conceded now that the building facing as it does an historical plain with such a beautiful prospect is in just the proper place.

The cry that it was so far away was met with the statement that the Buffalo Historical building is four miles from the centre of the city, that Dundurn Castle, the seat of the Wentworth Historical Society is over a mile away as is also the Peterboro Historical Society building. This change of site entailed the trouble of having three deeds made out, first, I gave one to my brother, second, he gave one to me, third, I gave one to the Historical Society.

At last, on April, 1906, the first sod was removed and the work at first progressed rapidly, but some delay occurred waiting for the Masons, maple flooring being lost in the way, waiting for the arrival of many things, but notwithstanding all those delays by the Fall of 1906, the building was finished except the portico which from the early frost could not be proceeded with.

With regard to the name the following words occurred in the circular sent out. "Several names have been suggested, "The U.E.L. Memorial," "Memorial of War of 1812," but a later suggestion is to call it simply Memorial Hall, it would thus be in memory of the U.E. Loyalists who landed here, and whose names may be inscribed on the walls, it may be in memory of Regiments, British and Canadian which have fought here, whose names may also find a place on the walls, or it may be in memory of the early settlers of whatever kind, or of the business men who helped to make Niagara an important Town, and in short it may be a memorial of whatever great or good has been done here in the past." And Memorial Hall it is. In the revolving case and on the wall are pictures of different kinds, oil paintings, water colors, silhouettes, ambrotypes of at least 300 of our early people, besides this another group of places, buildings, Military Clothing from the Revolutionary War indeed from the French occupation down to the Fenian Raid, nay even to the Boer War, another group of women's work and women's wear, articles of household economy whose use is unknown to many of our young people, Indian weapons and wear, early printing especially that done in our town. The building itself has in it several pieces of historic material, some oak, steps from Butler's Barracks, brick and stone from the Rogers store which wholesale house in 1833, supplied the stores for forty miles around our Town with goods. There is a Colonial Mantel or rather two, from old houses. We are to have a gavel made from the old Parliament Oak. The outside brick was furnished by A.W. Wright, Mimico, the hard Maple flooring from Meaford, the Georgia pine railing and Mahogany Posts from Cincinnati. The cases have been made from seasoned chestnut grown here, others obtained elsewhere are made of oak and walnut. Several cases have been contributed. The revolving case was made in England and presented to us. When the amount of $4,000 was reached, we received a cheque for $500 from an old Niagara boy, Hugh J. Chisholm, New York, which gladdened our hearts, as this would pay for the furnishing. Mr. Rittenhouse of Chicago also contributed $100 and last the Town Council $200. In writing letters asking for contributions it was found that our publications were of great assistance to us having awakened interest in our work. It must not be forgotten that the old boys of the High School have contributed generously. A registered letter containing $50 in bills was a pleasant surprise to us from an old gentleman whom we had not seen and who had, though a wealthy man, been solicited for contributions in his city, to Y.M.C.A. Library, Hospital and other worthy objects.

It is said it is well to have a friend at Court and it seems that we have been particularly fortunate in this respect and have had not one but many who have given us hints how and when and to whom to apply for assistance. It may be told at some other time how many circulars were sent out, how many contributors, how much from members of Society, at home and abroad, Dominion, Province, County Council, Township, Town, other friends.

Letters were written to the Colonels of the Regiments which had fought or been stationed here and from three of these contributions were sent, the Royal Scots, the 70th Surrey and the 5th Fusiliers stationed respectively in Scotland, India and England.

A word may be said as to the members of the committee who made all the arrangements as to the building. It was proposed to appoint a building committee but the work was principally done by a few of the original and as many of these were in Toronto and could not attend it devolved on those here and at last from different reasons the number dwindled down to three, Messrs. Alfred Ball, F.J. Rowland and myself, as Mr. Paffard removed to the Northwest and Mr. A. Servos has been long in ill health, both of whom had rendered efficient service, Mr. Kirby also was in poor health while the work was going on, but a small number on a committee can sometimes work together better than a large number. The only Toronto member who attended any of the Committee meeting was Mrs. Thompson who has taken much interest in the work and given valuable advice. There were in all twelve committee meetings. The first sod was turned in April, 1906, the building was finished all but the portico in October of that year. The cases were ready by February 1907 and we moved in February 4th, and the work of arrangement was commenced by Mrs. Thompson and myself the former having kindly offered help and to her we are deeply indebted for the assistance given during three weeks of the coldest weather of the winter. And again in May, she has also by her haste in arrangements put us under heavy obligations. There are now over 4,000 articles, the books and pamphlets themselves numbering 800, the newspapers 1,000, the pictures 500, Military 150, china 80, Indian 300, women's wear 150, miscellaneous 200, furniture 20. Besides this a large scrapbook relating to family records, municipal matters, churches; numbering 1,000 documents; many articles have a story and from our documents, we have been able frequently to answer letters asking for information.

Our members and contributors are in Manitoba, Scotland, England, New York, Chicago, West Indies, Savannah, India, South Africa, Calgary, etc. most remarkable coincidences have occurred in obtaining or giving information and, in acknowledgement of this, valuable books and pictures have often been sent to us. We exchange with thirty Historical Societies and thus are accumulating a valuable library. Our Societies are for States or Countries and it seemed a daring thing for a Town as small as ours to make such an attempt and indeed of our members, only a fifth are in Town and many of those absent in the winter when our meetings are held or are otherwise unable to attend, so that if we have had many encouragement's, we have also had difficulties with which to contend.

A word must be said as to the work, the contract was let to, Messrs. Carnochan & Dorritty, the mason work was given to Bennett of St. Catharines, cases were made by Mr. Jno. Carnochan assisted by W. Richardson, the painting and graining by Albert Davy, the hardware mostly procured in town, the metallic roofing from Toronto.

May the building continue to be in greater degree, a receptacle for anything pertaining to the history of our Country and while we acknowledge with gratitude, the help given and the success which has crowned our efforts we hope for still greater things in the future. We cordially thank all who have in any way, assisted, either in money, articles for the collection, time given, or advice and solicit a continuation of such favours.

A FEW OF THE MOST INTERESTING ARTICLES IN MEMORIAL HALL
Published in 1908
By Janet Carnochan

The question is frequently asked, what do you consider the most valuable article in the collection? This is not an easy question to answer, for there are so many valuable articles in the various divisions, Military, Literary, Artistic, Useful and the answer of different individuals would vary with the varying taste of the person interrogated. Whether General Brock's cocked hat, the first novel published in Upper Canada, or the first poem, the American Sword given up in 1812, the powder horn of Chief Brant, muster roll of Butler's Rangers, 1782, Library record book, 1800-1820, key of powder magazine, mahogany looking glass brought in 1784, the Empire dress, old flags, etc. in such an "embarrassment of riches" it is indeed difficult to decide. And then so many of the articles have a story connected with them. In our Number 5 is a short article, the "Evolution of an Historical Room." This is now out of print but when re-printed much may well be added as instead of the 1,000 articles then, there are now over 4,000.

How little valued generally is this common poster, and yet here are several which have fortunately been preserved and often settle some disputed point. Here on the wall facing General Brock's cocked hat, is the poster framed, printed by William Lyon McKenzie in Queenston of the arrangements for the re-interment of Brock in 1824, under the first monument, the body having lain for 12 years at Fort George, also after the arrangements for the final burial under the new monument in 1853. The cocked hat we must confess was never worn by the General as it came out shortly after his death and was given by the nephew to George Ball and is now placed here by a great grandson. Had it arrived earlier and been worn by the General, we should not be its fortunate possessors as all the clothing was sent home to the Island of Guernsey. A letter may be read in the life of the hero referring to the non-arrival of the cocked hat and the General's disappoint. Near this is the American Sword given up at he capture of Fort Niagara in December, 1813, after Niagara had been burned; this is loaned by A. Servos, Lake Road, a great-grandson of Lt. D.K. Servos to whom the sword was handed; a powder horn with Indian hieroglyphics given by Chief Brant to the Interpreter Jean Baptiste Rousseaux; a pewter platter part of the camp equipage of Col. Johnson killed at the siege of Fort Niagara 1759 and buried in the chapel with General Prideaux after the capture of the French by Sir Wm. Johnson; the coat worn by Fort Major Campbell who surrendered with Cornwallis at Yorktown in 1781; the poster proclamation issued by Wm. Lyon McKenzie from Navy Island in 1838 and another offering reward for the capture of Morreau who was hanged at Niagara the same year; a collection of Military Buttons, framed, which may be said to give the military history of Niagara, they representing nearly all the Regiments, British, United States, and Canadian, which fought or were stationed here. The coat, sash, powder horn, belt buckle of a member of that noted regiment of the King's Dragoon Guards here in 1838; various views of Niagara in 1794, 1813, 1824, 1846, nearly all being the original pencil sketch; a plan drawn for Mrs. Curzon showing the path of Laura Secord in her remarkable walk of twenty miles to warn the British at Beaver Dams; several valuable water color portraits by the celebrated Hoppner Meyer and several good oil paintings of early settlers; the Pocket book of Captain Marten McClellan who was killed at the capture of Fort George, 27th May, 1813; copies of the Upper Canada Gazette or American Oracle printed at Niagara, then Newark, 1794; a pamphlet also printed there in 1799; the first volume of the Gleaner, 1817; the first novel printed in Upper Canada in 1824 at Kingston, which is a very rare book; also the first poem, Wonders of the West or a Day at the Falls of Niagara, printed at York in 1825, an almanac printed at Rochester by W.L. Mackenzie when a prisoner in jail; Anti-Masonic almanacs of 1828-9, after the abduction of Morgan; sermons preached in Boston 1760 with thanksgiving for the victories of the British over the French in Canada and India; the Record book of the first Library in Upper Canada at Niagara 1800-1820, with the signature of proprietors; the hat worn by Ralfe Clench at the opening of Parliament here 17th September, 1792; pictures of two steamboats built for Hon. Jno. Hamilton, one the "Queenston" at Queenston 1824, and the other the "Great Britain" at Prescott in 1830; another famous old steam boat the "Chief Justice Robinson" which used to sail all winter, crossing from Toronto to Niagara; a beautiful banner made for the Grimsby Loyal and Patriotic Society for the inauguration of Brock's Monument in 1853; two flags presented by the Misses Nelles in 1818 to the 3rd Lincoln of which Robert Nelles was the Colonel. Also there was lent for us for the summer, the little silk Union Jack which was placed at the summit of the old Monument by a sailor lad who climbed by the lightning conductor of the tottering monument while thousands of spectators stood with bated breath fearing to see him fall, at the Indignation Meeting after the malicious shattering of the Monument with gunpowder. The old mantel with the ancient crane, waffle iron, warming pan, tinder box, foot warmer to take to Church, or the Colonial mantel of 1812, opposite, the evolving case of pictures of early settlers copied from silhouettes, ambrotypes, water colors, oil paintings, Secord, Servos, Ball, Whitmore, Clench, Field, Cooper, etc. and in more modern times, the Doctors, Clergymen, Mayors, Judges, Members of Parliament of the Town. Hanging in the gallery is the figure of an angel blowing a trumpet, which was the weather vane of St. Andrew's Church in 1831, but when a tornado took off the roof in 1854, the vane was twisted and lay in a Painter's Shop for nearly fifty years and finally was brought here. A round table in two parts, belonged to the Secord family for over a hundred years, a wicker work chair was owned by Rev. Jno. Burns, one of the first Ministers of St. Andrew's a century ago. A high post bedstead, house fire engine, cannon balls which came over in 1812-13, not as messengers of love. A bound volume of the Gleaner for 1831-2, another has specimens from fourteen of the twenty newspapers published in the Town from 1793 to the present time.

Quite the oldest things in the room are some beautifully shaped flint arrow heads used by the Britons before the Saxons came, also a Roman Battle Axe found in a Ayrshire Bog. A Sepoy sword, also a Waterloo sword, a Cavalry bit is a relic of the American Occupation in 1813, as also a canteen with the letters U.S. Philadelphia. A large scrap book has many interesting documents, a list of Indian Sachems and Warriors who presented 15,000 acres of land to Col. William Claus, and elopement letter of 1801 and a love letter of 1824, a curious list of burial expenses in Queenston, 1817, the amount and variety of liquor used is astounding, port wine, brandy, gin, Stout, Madeira wine, Teneriffe wine amounting in all with digging the grave to 12 pounds, 2 shillings.

The list of Sunday School scholars who gave 7?, ls, 3d, 2s, 6d, respectively to provide a chair for the old clerk who had served for fifty years at St. Mark's; the Petition to the Queen from heads of families in St. Andrew's in 1842 re: Clergy Reserves, a beautiful water color of roses, executed by Mrs. Moodie, the author of *Roughing in the Bush*. A sampler with the words, God Save the King, G.R. III by Margaret Stewart in 1812; the photo of a sampler worked in the winter of 1812-13 by Mrs. Denison, nee Lippincott, in memory of Sir Isaac Brock with the words, "Push on York Volunteers" showing that this is not a modern story as some have asserted. A tuning box made in 1847 for St. Andrew's Church, Embroidery done in 1815 by a daughter of Dominic Henry, the Light House Keeper, original letters of Allan MacNab, Samuel Street, Alexander McLeod, Jas. Crooks, etc.; beautiful pieces of ancient china and also embroidery, autographs of Secretary Jarvis, Governor Simcoe, Ralfe Clench, Isaac Swayze, Col. Butler, Judge Hamilton, etc.

Military commissions of Robert Nelles, Jas. Clement, Cortlandt Secord with signatures of governors as Peregrine Maitland, Colborne, Gore, Russell. An old gun called the Indian Chief, a flintlock of 1812, a Fenian Raid gun and our latest contribution a Boer gun with its original owner's name.

A word must be said as to the largest contributors to the collections and indeed without whose aid our room would not present the appearance it fortunately does, Charles A.F. Ball has been very generous in documents, old newspapers, books, household articles, also Alfred Ball, Mrs. J.E. Wilson, Toronto; Mrs. J.G. Currie, St. Catharines, Mrs. Alfred Ball, Mrs. Camidge, Mrs. Chas. A.F. Ball, Miss Gilkison, Brantford; Alexander Servos; John A. Blake, John Carnochan; Mrs. George A. Clement; Herbert Blake; Miss E. Campbell, Toronto; Collin Milloy; Miss Minnie Ball, John Ross Robertson, Toronto; Johnson Clench, St. Catharines: M.G. Scherk, Toronto; Miss Claus; Miss Green; Mrs. John Secord; Richard Taylor; David Boyle, Toronto; Henry Paffard; Dr. Millroy, Scotland; Miss Flanigan, Mrs. Newton, Miss Emma Ball, Mrs. John Carnochan, Miss Stewart, Toronto; Mrs. W. Richardson, Miss Crouch, Virgil; Mrs. Peckham, Toledo; Miss Cathline, Miss Dreger, Mrs. Radcliff, Miss Miller, Newbury; the Educational Department in discarded cases and many others.

2007 Niagara Historical Society

Honorary Life Members

Wilfred Agnes
Joy Ormsby
Richard Taylor

Board of Directors

Kelly James, President
Donna Scott, VP Society
Jim Armstrong, VP Museum
Barbara McCarthy, Secretary
Daryl Novak, Treasurer
Lois Chapman
Harry Murdoch
David Murray
Deborah Paine-Corbiere
Andrew Panko

Staff

Clark Bernat, Managing Director
Amy Klassen, Society Administrator

Niagara Historical Society Presidents

1895-1925	Janet Carnochan
1925-1951	C.H.E. Smith
1951-1952	Ernest E. Melville
1952-1955	George Carnochan
1955-1957	J.I. Gordon
1957-1959	C.N.P. Blagrave
1959-1961	Brain Doherty
1961-1963	Ross A. Short
1963-1968	Jack Dorland
1968-1970	Brigadier W.J. Moogk
1970-1971	Francis R. Kirton
1971-1973	Ann Stokes
1973-1975	Paul Johns
1975-1977	John L. Field
1977-1978	Gwen O'Loughlin
1978-1980	Russell L. Netherton
1980-1982	Keith Campbell
1982-1983	Frank Hawley
1983-1985	Norman Green
1985-1989	Nancy Butler
1989-1992	Dr. Richard Merritt
1992-1994	Clifford James
1994-1996	Wilfrid M. Agnes
1996-1998	David E. Ker
1998-2000	Les Taylor
2000-2003	Sheila Tierney
2003-2007	Kelly James

Other Books by the Niagara Historical Society

Publication Title
The Battle of Fort George
Centennial Poem, Fort Niagara
The Blockade of Fort George, The Battle of Stoney Creek, U.E. Loyalists, History Taught in Museums, Queenston Heights, Monuments
Rev. Addison, Mrs. Rousseaux, Historic Houses, Historic Room
Niagara Library 1800 to 1820, Early School of Niagara
Historic Forts, Churches, Houses
Family History of Servos, Whitmore, Jarvis and Land
Campaigns of 1812 to 1814
Inscriptions and Graves in the Niagara Peninsula
Reminiscences of Niagara
The Battle of Fort George
Canadian Heroine, Historic House, Names Only, St. Vincent de Paul
Letters of Mrs. Wm. Dummer Powell 1607 - 1821
Sir Isaac Brock, Count de Puisaye, Tributes to Mrs. Green and William Kirby
Report of the Opening of Memorial Hall
Ten Years of the Colony of Niagara 1780 - 1790
Early History of St. Mark's, Robert Gourlay
Reminiscences of Fenian Raid, St. Davids, Confederation, Boucherville Journal
Some Graves in Lundy's Lane
Fort Niagara, 1612 Letters, The Steamer Chicora
Catalogue of Articles in Memorial Hall 1911
Laura Secord, Monument at Lundy's Lane, Queenston, Red River
Notes on the History of the District of Niagara 1791 - 1793
Names Only but much more, No. 1 Company Niagara
Family History and Reminiscences of Early Settlers
The Niagara Frontier 1837 to 1838
<u>Some Notable Results of the War, Hon. William Dickson</u>
Letters of 1812, Brock's Monument, W.J. Wright, Burying Grounds
Notes on Niagara 1759 - 1860
Notes on the Invasion of the Niagara Peninsula
Whose Debtors We Are
Capt. Hamilton, Polish Forces, Rev. Addison, Rev. Burns
Fifty Years of Peach Culture, Simcoe, Queenston, Goring, Secords, Decew

U.E. Loyalists, Kirby, Rev. Hooker, Read, The Women's Institute

Records of Niagara 1778 to 1783

Records of Niagara 1784 to 1787

Records of Niagara 1784 to 1789

Records of Niagara 1790 to 1792

Records of Niagara 1805 to 1811

Records of Niagara 1812 to 1813

Records of Niagara 1813 January to July

Shipwrecked on Sable Island

The Capital Years (Dundurn Press)

Stones, Saints and Sinners

Slavery & Freedom

The Friendly Invasion

Niagara-on-the-Lake (Vanwell Publishing)

Niagara-on-the-Lake as a Confederate Refuge (Nicholas Rescher and the Niagara Historical Society)

The Forgotten Story of an Old Town Pottery (Monica and Richard Taylor)